Thomas Mitchell

The Sword of Truth. Christ and Paul-Socrates and Plato-Which?

Future punishment: Biblical, scientific and philosophic

Thomas Mitchell

The Sword of Truth. Christ and Paul-Socrates and Plato-Which?
Future punishment: Biblical, scientific and philosophic

ISBN/EAN: 9783337101787

Printed in Europe, USA, Canada, Australia, Japan

Cover: Foto ©Lupo / pixelio.de

More available books at **www.hansebooks.com**

THE
Sword of Truth.

Christ and Paul—Socrates and Plato—
WHICH?

Future Punishment:
Biblical, Scientific and Philosophic.

Endless Misery and Purgatorial Restoration:
Myths of Heathenism.

WHAT IS TRUTH?

"See, I have set before thee this day, life and good, and, death and evil."—Deut. xxx, 15.

BY
Prof. THOMAS MITCHELL,
OF
THE BIBLICAL AND SCIENTIFIC COLLEGE,
BROOKLYN, N. Y.

AUTHOR OF

"*Philosophy of God and the World,*" "*The Gospel Crown of Life,*" "*The Old Paths,*" "*Philosophy of Spiritualism, (No Spirits,)*" "*Household Tragedy,*" (*A Poem,*) "*Voices from Paradise,*" (*A Poem,*) "*The True and False Church,*" "*Commentary on the Book of Revelation,*" "*Civil and Religious Liberty,*" "*Darwinism and the Geological Antiquity of Man, refuted by Philosophy, Science and the Bible,*" "*Phonetic and Stenographic Short Hand,*" "*Water Baptism No Ordinance of the Christian Church.*"

BROOKLYN, N. Y.:
H. R. STARKWEATHER, PRINTER, 235 ADELPHI STREET.
1878.

Entered according to Act of Congress, in the year 1878, by

THOMAS MITCHELL, The Author,

in the Office of the Librarian of Congress, at Washington.

INTRODUCTION.

AT a recent meeting of the New York Synod of the Reformed Episcopal Church, comprising the States of New York, New Jersey and Connecticut, on a discussion of a resolution relating to eternal, conscious torment, Dr. Leacock said, "That if the Church failed to adopt the resolution it would go down. Eternal punishment was the foundation of all grace." Dr. Sabine said, "That they could not consult their own feelings in the doctrine of eternal punishment. They all wished that after-punishment would not be eternal, but they should be guided by the word of God." The resolution was, "Whether they believe that the punishment of the wicked is eternal and conscious."

We do not quote their opinions in our Introduction because of the prominence of the individuals enunciating them, but because they give expression to a common absurdity and a common wish connected with the doctrine of "Endless misery." The absurdity is, that eternal punishment is the foundation of all grace.

Now, if such is the truth, then there is the same relation and connection between the punishment and the grace as between the foundation of a house and the house built thereon—without the one the other has no existence; the house, therefore, being built upon the foundation, is *of the foundation*, and so the grace is *of the punishment*. It is proper, therefore, to read all the passages of Scripture containing the word "grace," with the qualifying words "Eternal punishment" before them. It must also be remembered that grace means "favor," "a free gift." Paul had a thorn in the flesh, the messenger of satan, to buffet him, and for his encouragement God says to him, "My grace is sufficient for you," and according to Dr. Leacock He should have said, "Paul, My grace of eternal punishment is sufficient for you, which I will freely give unto you, and it is to be inflicted by satan, who will buffet you without any end."

"The grace of God, that bringeth salvation, hath appeared unto all men." The new reading would be, "God's grace or free gift of *eternal punishment*, that bringeth salvation, hath appeared unto all men." "Be sober and hope unto the end for the grace that is to be brought unto us at the appearing of Jesus Christ." The new version would read it, "Hope unto the end for the grace of eternal punishment which is to be brought unto us at the appearing of Jesus Christ, which He will freely give unto us." "The grace of our Lord Jesus Christ be with you all, Amen." The reformed reading would be, "The grace of eternal punishment be with you all, Amen, which He shall freely give unto you."

That it was the wish of that whole Synod that future

punishment was not eternal, as declared by Dr. Sabine, we cannot but have our doubts, and that they only yielded to it because it is taught by the Word of God. If they were as willing that the Word of God should not teach it as that it does teach it, why did they add to the Word of God the qualifying word "conscious," to those of eternal punishment, in their resolution? That all the advocates of endless misery add words to those of the Words of God, it seems to us betrays a sectarian bias and determination to adhere to the heathen dogma at all hazards, utterly disqualifying them to reason upon the questions involved. Indeed, this hallucination impells them on in the fearful work of changing the Words of God under the pretense of believing them, which amounts to infatuation, making them teach exactly opposite ideas, turning as deaf an ear to the following fearful warning as though it was not in the Bible: "For I testify unto every man that heareth the words of the prophesy of this Book, if any man shall add unto these things, God shall add unto him the plagues that are written in this Book; and if any man shall take away from the words of the Book of this prophesy, God shall take away his part out of the Book of life, and out of the Holy City, and from the things which are written in this Book."—Rev. xxii, 18, 19.

Let us introduce some examples to show how the advocates of endless misery thus take away and add to the words of the Book of God. Endless punishment implies eternal life, but there is not one passage in the Bible which says the wicked have or ever shall have eternal or everlasting life. Nor is there a single passage which says man's soul or spirit is by nature immortal or immortal at all; but conscious torment renders its possession indispensable, as a being must live, in order to be conscious, and he must be conscious in order to suffer; and if the suffering is endless, his life and consciousness must be also eternal. On the other hand, eternal life is promised to the righteous and is conferred alone by Jesus Christ. And we may add that these terms mean nothing more than conscious existence—not happiness; not misery; these are additionally promised and threatened to the righteous and the wicked, and of themselves imply existence, but not duration. Immortality or eternal life simply gives the qualification to suffer or enjoy, but is no part of either. If the words endless punishment, endless suffering or endless misery were in the Bible, that would end the controversy to the satisfaction of all who received it as the Word of God; but when men are obliged to add these in order to make it teach their doctrine, and call the unholy "*Babel*" the Word of God, what else does it exhibit but the most "deceitful handling of the Word of God," and how can such men honestly declare they wish future punishment was not eternal? If they really desired the punishment of the wicked not to be endless, would they not be willing to quote the Words of God without qualifying terms added, to make them state the fact with the utmost positiveness, which otherwise could admit of nothing but inferences in its support? To make out this doctrine they are not only obliged to add qualifying terms, but those which convey exactly opposite ideas.

To illustrate this perversion of the Word of God we will introduce a few examples: "Fear Him which is able to destroy both soul and body in hell."—Matt. x, 28. Quoting from Aristotle, Socrates and Plato, in answer to this, they say, "Jesus, you are mistaken; the soul is immortal, and therefore you nor your Father are able to destroy it. It is absolutely indestructable; so, sinners, you need not fear such a penalty." What you should have said, was, that He intended to preserve—not destroy—the soul and body both, in hell. Indeed, I made it so that I cannot destroy the soul if I would. Here we have the nonsense that any being cannot unmake what he made, supposing him not to have lost his mind or power. "The Lord Jesus shall be revealed from heaven with His mighty angels, in flaming fire, taking vengeance on them that know not God, and obey not the gospel of our Lord Jesus Christ, who shall be punished with everlasting destruction."—2 Thess. i, 8, 9. This is an error of materialism, Paul, the soul is the man proper, and being immaterial and immortal, it is absolutely indestructable.

"For God so loved the world, that He gave His only begotten Son, that whosoever believeth in Him should not perish, but have everlasting life." This means that whosoever disbelieves in Christ, and spurns the love of God, shall never perish, but have everlasting life; indeed, the wicked are imperishable. "But the wicked shall perish, and the enemies of the Lord shall be as fat of lambs; they shall consume; into smoke shall they consume away."—Ps. xxxvii, 20. This means they shall never consume at all, for if they consumed in the least degree there would come a time when they would cease to exist, and this would contradict Plato, who says they are immortal, and, therefore, it cannot be true.

"Behold, the day cometh that shall burn as an oven; and all the proud, yea, and all that do wickedly, shall be stubble; and the day that cometh shall burn them up, saith the Lord of hosts, that it shall leave them neither root nor branch."—Mal. iv, 1. All we have to say about this passage is that it is poetry, or highly strung figurative speech. To represent the wicked as being as combustable as stubble, when the heathen philosophers declare them immortal, imperishable and indestructable, would be to become a materialist.

"He that being often reproved, hardeneth his neck, shall suddenly be destroyed, and that without remedy." Prov. xxix, 1. The wicked cannot be destroyed, the remedy against it is, that they are immortal, and therefore indestructible. "For the day of the Lord is near, upon all the heathen, and they shall be as though they had not been."—Obadiah, 15, 16. This passage is a wrong translation, it should have been, "The wicked *shall always be*," for their existence is endless. "The soul that sinneth, it shall die."—Ez. xviii, 4. This passage also is a bad translation. It should have been rendered, "The soul that sinneth, it shall never die," and this would also suit our beautiful hymn:

> "A *never-dying soul* to save
> And fit it for the sky."

In view of taking such liberty with the production of a human author, is it possible that any respect for him should be felt, or any fear of consequences? And if the same course is persued with the teachings of the Bible by any man, is it possible for him to have the least realization that an infinitely wise Being is its author, or that man is to be judged by His Words at the last day? Christ said, "The words that I have spoken unto you they shall judge you in the last day." What such men say, in fact, is, that the doctrines taught by Aristotle, Socrates and Plato, relating to the immortality of the soul and future punishment, are orthodox, while Jesus and Paul, and all who believe their doctrines upon these subjects, are heretics, and the system is a low species of materialism. A little girl said, "Mamma, If God did not mean what He said, why did He not tell us what He did mean?" It would be well for the Doctors to take the rebuke.

That our readers may not be intimidated by the cheap parrot cry of "Heresy," from the reception of Bible truth, let us briefly consider it. There are but two passages in the Scriptures which show in what heresy consists. These relate to Christ's death and resurrection. One is brought out in Paul's defence before Felix and Agrippa. Says the Apostle, " Neither can they prove the things whereof they accuse me; but this I confess unto thee, that after the way which they call heresy, so worship I the God of my fathers, believing all things which are written in the law and in the prophets; and have hope toward God, which they themselves also allow, that there shall be a resurrection of the dead, both of the just and unjust. Let these say if they have found any evil doings in me, except, while I stood before the council, it be for this one voice that I cried, standing among them, touching the resurrection of the dead," (for which) " I am called in question by you this day; and now I stand, and am judged for the hope of the promise made of God unto our fathers; unto which promise, our twelve tribes, instantly serving God day and night, hope to come. For which hope's sake, King Agrippa, I am accused ot the Jews. Why should it be thought a thing incredible with you, that God should raise the dead? For these causes the Jews caught me in the temple, and went about to kill me; having therefore obtained help of God, I continue unto this day, witnessing both to small and great, saying none other things than those which the Prophets and Moses did say should come; that Christ should suffer, and that He should be the first that should rise from the dead."—Acts xxiv, 13—15, 21, chapter xxvi, 6—8, 21—23.

It is certain from this that the doctrine that Christ died and rose again, is not heresy, or Paul was a heretic. Neither is it the death and resurrection of the *body* that constitutes this doctrine. What is called "The Apostle's creed," but which contains the Papal heresy that the death of Christ or the saints was nothing but separation, in the words, "I believe in the resurrection of the *body*." The Papists had adopted the heathen doctrine of Aristotle and Plato, that the soul, or spirit, was immortal, and was the man proper, applying it equally to Christ, and defining it to be the living, feeling, thinking, intellectual being who dwelt in the mortal, material body as its house. Hence, Christ did not and could not have died. And as the material, mortal body was no part of the living inhabitant, neither could it die; therefore, there was no death of Christ at all, and if there was no death there could have been no resurrection of the dead, as that which did not die could not be raised from the dead.

We have, however, seen that it was Christ himself who suffered, died and rose again from the dead, and not merely His body, as it is expressed. It is evident from this, that it was the Jews themselves who were the heretics, and not Paul, and that the heresy consisted in the denial of the resurrection of the dead. The other passage is as follows: "But there were false Prophets' (teachers) "also among the people, even as there shall be false teachers among you, who privily shall bring in damnable heresies, even denying the Lord that bought them, and bring upon themselves swift destruction, and many shall follow their pernicious ways, by reason of whom the way of truth shall be evil spoken of."—2 Pet. ii, 1, 2.

That the death and resurrection of Christ, not His body, is the price by which the salvation of men becomes possible, are the very foundation-truths of Christianity. Hence, there are scores of such passages as these: "Ye are bought with a price."—1 Cor. vi, 20. "Christ died for us."—Rom. v, 8. It was Christ, not His body, that died. "For as much as ye know that ye were not redeemed with corruptable things, as silver and gold, but with the precious blood of Christ."—1 Pet. i, 18, 19. It was not with the precious blood of His body, but with Christ himself, "Which none of the princes of this world knew; for had they known, they would not have crucified the Lord of glory,"—1 Cor. ii, 8. Here we see it was the Lord of glory, and not simply the lowest, dead, material part of Him, which was crucified.

"And the angel answered and said unto the woman, fear ye not, for I know that ye seek Jesus, which was crucified; He is not here, for He is risen, as He said. Come, see the place where the Lord lay."—Matt. xxviii, 5, 6. Here it was Jesus who was crucified, and not His body—the house in which He lived. It was the Lord himself who had laid dead in the tomb, and not simply the material body in which He had resided, and out of which He had moved, never having died at all. In fact, being immortal, He could not have died; Christ the Lord, therefore, cheated death, and never died for sinners. and hence, they cannot be saved. This is the "damnable heresy," Paul said should come, "denying the Lord that bought them." And Jesus going up to Jerusalem, took the twelve disciples apart in the way, and said unto them, behold, we go up to Jerusalem; and the Son of Man shall be betrayed unto the chief priests, and unto the scribes, and they shall condemn Him to death and shall crucify Him, and the third day He shall rise again."—Matt. xx, 17, 19. Here Jesus himself was to be crucified, killed, and rise from the dead the third day, and not His body merely, which was only a part of Himself. The living, feeling, thinking part was not to live on as though nothing had happened, thus cheating death of its prey, and by this monster heresy of the world, failing to redeem men by His death and resurrection.

It is the doctrine of the natural immortality of the soul of Christ and that of His saints, which renders His death and resurrection, and their death and resurrection, impossibilities, and is, therefore, the most damnable heresy ever introduced into the world, giving man eternal life through the first Adam, by natural transmission, leaving Christ, the second Adam, nothing to do. As this was the great object for which He was given, and to be accomplished by the love of God, thus expressed: "God so loved the world that He gave His only begotten Son, that whosoever believeth in Him should not perish, but have everlasting life." The heathens respond to God, "You might have saved your love, and to Christ, you might have avoided your sufferings, if you had understood Aristotle,

Socrates and Plato, who could have informed you that all men have eternal life, immortal souls, already."

In the estimation of the Jews, all Christians are heretics. In that part of Roman Catholicism, all Protestants are heretics, and in the estimation of Protestants, all Jews and Catholics are heretics. In the sub-division of these, all are heretical to each other, each creed being the standard of orthodoxy, expelling members for not believing these, and forbidding them to appeal to the Bible as authority in making their defence. In view of such facts, we hold it to be a very high recommendation to be called a heretic by Jews, Catholics and Protestants, and any man thus stigmatized, may exultingly exclaim with Paul, "After the manner which they call heresy, so worship I the God of my fathers," "Calling no man master but Christ." The cry of heresy is, in our day, as harmless against those who appeal alone to the Holy Scriptures for their doctrines

"As a tale told by an idiot, full
Of sound and fury, signifying nothing."

"He who cannot reason is a fool; he who dare not reason is a bigot, but he who reasons freely is a man."

TABLE OF CONTENTS.

The Times Favorable for the Discussion................... 19
Advocates of Eternal Torments, Embarrassed............. 20
The Notion of Going to Heaven at Death, not True......... 21
The Hypothesis of Purgatorial Restoration, Unreasonable and Unscriptural..................................... 23
A Proud Sinner in Heaven 25
Endless Misery the most Unphilosophic and Unscriptural of all Other Theories................................. 26
The Punishment, a Guilty Conscience, Absurd............ 29
The Hypothesis Offers Great Reward Instead of Punishment 31
The True Hypothesis, Extinction of Conscious Being...... 32
The Question Dividing the Subject, Sin and Death......... 34
Why the World was Cursed.............................. 35
The Devil, Sinners and Sin, Doomed to Destruction........ 37
Man Lost Everlasting Life when he Sinned................ 39
Destruction Always Without End......................... 40
Hell, the Grave, and the Hell of Future Punishment........ 41
The Terms Describing the Punishment.................... 42
The Place where the Wicked were Consumed, an Eternal Monument.. 43
Wicked Men and Devils Punished on the Earth........... 45
The Location of Hell..................................... 45
The Quenchless Fires Go Out............................ 49
The Great Contest between Christ and the Wicked at the Last Day.... 50
The Infliction of the Second Death....................... 53
Wicked Wresting of the Scriptures....................... 55
Scripture Testimony that the Wicked will be Destroyed.... 56
The Worm shall not Die.................................. 60

The Smoke of their Torment Goes Out	62
The Meaning of the Words Forever and Ever not Necessarily Endless	62
This Discussion a Subject of Prophesy Connected with the Coming of Christ	66
Limitation of the Word Everlasting	67
The Words "Vengeance of Eternal Fire," not Endless Misery	69
A Three-fold Argument	70
Origin of the Doctrine of Endless Torments, Heathen Philosophy	71
Socrates on Immortality	73
Socrates went to Heaven at Death	75
How the Heathen Doctrine of Endless Misery Came into the Church	75
Catholicism Founded on Heathenism	78
Socrates did not Die, he only Moved out of his Body; but Jesus did die	79
The Doctrine of Immortality by Christ in the Resurrection, Fatal to Romanism	81
The Origin of Purgatory	83
Heathen Future Punishment, Adopted by Protestantism	84
The Heresy of Exalting Satan to be Christ's Compeer	86
Eternal Misery Forbids the Possibility of Loving God	87
God's Ministers and Plato's	91
Eternal Life Offered to the Righteous	92
Heathenism Knew Nothing of the Immortality of the Gospel	94
No Rewards or Punishments till the Resurrection at the Last Day	95
The Saints not to be with the Lord, Until He Comes Again	97
What Things are Subjects of God's Decrees	98
This not a New Doctrine	99
The Immortal Change of the Living Saints at the Last Day	100
The Two Adams—One Giving Death, the Other, Life	101
The Platonic Distribution of Souls	101
Death not Death, but Separation—a Doctrine of the Devil	102
Consciousness After Death, Wholly Supported by Inference. Location of Paradise	104
The Transfiguration, a Vision of Final Glory Beyond the Resurrection	112

When are the Saints the Children of God?	114
How to Determine the Chronology of Events	116
Elijah Died, in Common with all Men	117
Enoch Died also, and awaits his Resurrection and Translation	118
No Man Ever Went to God in Heaven	120
The Laws of Physiology and the Bible, Harmonize	121
Physiology Connected with this Question	121
What is the Soul?	122
What is the Meaning of Spirit?	124
Objection, "Lord Jesus, Receive my Spirit," Considered	127
Wind, Breath, and Spirit, Mean the Same	128
Etymology of the Word Spirit	130
Thought Depends Upon Life, Life Upon Organization	131
All the Vital Organs, Parts of Life	132
The Immortality of the Soul, Shown to be absurd by the Word of God	135
That the Spirit is Immortal, also Shown to be absurd by the Scriptures	139
No Future Punishment for the Heathen.–The Principle Stated	143
The Heathen Suffer the First Death, but Not the Second	147
The Conditions of Salvation or Eternal Life	150
The Place and Nature of the Promised Reward	152
Dr. Edward Beecher's Criticism on the Words *Aei* and *Aionios*	153
Reason for Introducing these Opinions	156
Objection, "This View Takes Away the Motive to Repentance," Answered	157
God's Oath in Contrast to the Picture of Horror	162
The Heathen Doctrine of Future Punishment Denies Christ's Death and Resurrection	163
An Appeal to the Corruptors of God's Words	165

Christ and Paul or Socrates and Plato —
WHICH ?

———•———

THE TIMES FAVORABLE FOR THE DISCUSSION.

We were engaged in writing an Exegesis or Commentary on the Book of Revelation, and had advanced to the words, "That thou shouldst destroy them which destroy the earth," as the last event of the seventh trumpet—chapter xi, verse 18, when the subject of future punishment sprang up, about a year ago, as by the touch of the Almighty, and from the grave of silence, wherein it had been interred for the last twenty-five years, and we determined to give it a thorough investigation, selecting that relating to it from the manuscript, and to have it published in the present form.

That the majority of the ministers of the present day have come into the pulpit during this period, leaves them less committed upon the subject of any particular views, and thereby better qualified for impartial investigation, in consequence of which there is much of the best talent of the United States and England defending the doctrine of the utter extermination of the wicked, and if not associated with the heathen, philosophic notion of the natural immortality of the soul, there is not a scholar in either country who would not adopt this view of the subject. It is plainly evident that the advocates of eternal, conscious torments, find themselves embarrassed at every point of the discussion concerning its nature and duration, and are obliged to have recourse to a system of interpretation of Bible language, which would be considered the work of a magician if applied to any other book, and utterly unworthy the honest student of the Word of God.

The Advocates of Eternal Torments Embarrassed.

According to it, destruction means, endless preservation; fire and brimstone, a guilty conscience; forever, absolutely endless; death means eternal life. It also compels them to contend for such incongruities, and even absurdities, as the following: That though God made the soul, He cannot unmake or destroy it. That the wicked, having gone, immediately at death, into hell, are taken out at the judgment, tried for the deeds they had done while living upon earth, for which some of them had been suffering already six thousand years, and then remanded back to their spiritual prison, there not to die, but to live forever. That the devil is now in hell, and yet he is going about like a roaring lion, seeking whom he may devour on earth. That though it is plainly declared Christ is to destroy the devil himself, and also his works, sin and sinners, he is going to do no such thing, but to preserve and perpetuate both, the sin to be without end, that He may be justified in punishing the sinner for the same duration. That the devil, the wickedest sinner of all, and God's greatest enemy, is to be exalted, to be hell's king, reigning most despotically over as many subjects as can be counted in Christ's kingdom, the victims of his malicious hate and cruelty, and but for whom they would have been in

Christ's own kingdom. Such are some of the sophistries and rediculous attitudes the defence of this old, foolish, heathen mythology compels the wise divines of the nineteenth century to assume.

THAT ALL GO TO HEAVEN AT DEATH, OR AT ALL, EXPLODED.

In relation to future punishment, there are, at the present day, four hypotheses. One of these claims that all go to heaven as soon as they die, entirely without regard to their moral character; the murderer, the suicide, the gambler, the drunkard, and the most grossly sunken in sin and vice; all; all ascend from the slums of iniquity, to mingle promiscuously with the purest human saints, angels and God. In regard to this theory, we may just remark, for it needs but a remark to dispose of it, that its injustice to the righteous, the moral similitude of virtue and God, puts it out of the controversy. According to the law of human nature and society, men seek congeniality of mental and moral qualities, and the highest type of Christian virtue are the most pained, when, by any circumstances, they are forced into the social circles of the low and vicious. In the present world, they may be spared such punishment by shunning the contact; but this theory forces those who have made the greatest attainments in assimilation to the Great Model himself, to associate in close companionship with all the vileness gathered from the earth. It is true and magnanimous that these highest, as did Christ himself, mingle with the very lowest in order to elevate and save, but now all are in heaven and beyond the possibility of moral reformation. They have passed the chronological period, when it had been said, "He that is unjust, let him be unjust still; and he which is filthy, let him be filthy still; and he that is righteous, let him be righteous still; and he that is holy, let him be holy still. And behold, I come quickly; and My reward is with Me, to give to every man according as his work shall be. I am Alpha and Omega, the beginning and the end, the first and the last. Blessed are they that do His commandments, that they may have right to the tree of life, and may enter in through the gates into the city; for with out, are dogs, and sorcerers, and whore-mongers, and murderers, and idolaters, and whosoever loveth and maketh a lie."—Rev. xxii, 11—15. Hence, the Word of God is in bold contrast to this doctrine. In contradiction to this, if it be claimed that the highest would reform the lowest by mingling together in heaven, we answer, if it had failed on earth, where such society existed, that is, where the virtuous were, but whose company was shunned by the wicked, except for the purpose of robbery and murder, why should it succeed any better in any other place?—transportation does not affect moral character. It must be granted that where a very small number of vicious men, placed into a society, composed say of ninety-five per cent. of the most virtuous, they would grow like them; but the fact is quite otherwise, showing that the vast majority who have lived and died are of the character here mentioned by the Revelator, and as the philosophy of this principle operates both ways, the wicked would be more likely to seduce and corrupt the lesser number of the righteous, and convert all into haters of God's righteous government, just as they are now in the world. The best that could be realized in such a state of things, where the two extremes meet, would be a compromise of virtue and vice—a lowering of the standard of holiness to accommodate, and, to an extent, to elevate the low, but which would compel God to banish the whole sin-loving company from His presence and dominions. In the very nature of things, therefore, God would cease to be God were He to admit the wicked into heaven; and for the very reason that He would be unjust to the righteous in punishing them with such painful association, as well as rendering them liable to contamination from the surrounding evil examples. Let it be remembered, also, that the advocates of this theory call the present world, hell, and the wicked, devils, because of the existence of this vicious character, and to transport it to any other place would it not be hell, still, and the actors, devils still; and if to heaven, would it not become hell itself? Behold, the conclusion of the universal-salvation hypothesis! Let the highest Angel in heaven leave his abode and continue to associate with his fallen companions, and he, too, would become a devil. To suppose such a system was taught in the Bible, and that God was its author, presents the most unphilosophic thought that ever floated through a human brain. No!

> "Vice is a monster of so great a mien,
> To be hated needs but to be seen;
> Yet, seen too oft', familiar with his face,
> We first endure, then pity, then embrace."
> —*Pope.*

THE HYPOTHESIS OF RESTORATION OR PURGATORY UNREASONABLE AND UNSCRIPTURAL.

The second hypothesis is, that all sinners are pardoned and purefied in the next world, in a kind of purgatorial half-way house, in which there are various apartments to suit the standards of sinners entering, each one as soon as he dies, as well as degrees of punishment through which all pass to fit them for heaven. This is the doctrine of the Catholic Church, and all the modifications of restorationism, including the Spiritualist, who fully adopts the doctrine of Socrates of natural immortality, bodiless spirits and purgatory, even to the idea that some are so vicious that they will never reach the society of the gods. In regard to this theory, we may say that all the objections we have offered against the other are more fatal to this, for in this future world of punishment, all are wicked, all are vicious, and not a good example for imitation to virtue existing; therefore, in the very nature of things, all must remain vicious, and grow more so, no matter what might be the wish of any for elevation; no power could exist for its indulgence or practice amid the surrounding downward gravities. Besides this, it must be remembered that no one is estimated virtuous, and a fit subject for God's kingdom, but those who love Him from the heart. Now, let it be proclaimed in purgatory, that every one, as soon as they are punished, so that they thus love the punisher, will be immediately released and admitted into His heavenly abode, how many would ever be qualified to fulfill the condition. It is true, many, and perhaps all, might be induced to profess to love Him, in order to escape further torments, but this would only add to their guilt the sin of heartless hypocrisy. This might defy the eye of man to detect, as he judges from appearances, but could not deceive the God whose eye looks into the heart, perceives its motives, discerns the intentions and most secret thoughts, taking cognizance of what the man is, and not what he may profess to be. How long, for illustration, would you have to burn a man, either in literal or spiritual fire, to make him love you? But you might induce him to beg your forgiveness, or to make any kind of promises to do service for you, to release himself from further punishment, and if released, to fulfill them all; but to make him love you is not in his power; indeed, it would tantalize him with the unreasonable demand and impossible duty, and would make him hate you still more. Hence, the spurious philosophy of the purgatorial fires, or any species of punishment, for the accomplishment of such an end.

A Proud Sinner in Heaven.

Besides, if it were true, it would set aside all mercy and grace, the most prominent principles of God's revealed plan of salvation. Those who had been punished to the full demerit of their crimes, would come up and demand admission into heaven on strictly legal grounds, asking no favors of saints, angels, Christ or God. He says, open the golden gate; I have paid the full penalty justice demanded; I care nothing for God; He punished me all the time, and to the full extent, in degree, justice would permit, and I am under no obligation to Him; I sing no songs in glorification of Christ, and His sufferings or sympathies for me; I have never humiliated myself to repentance or confession; I have asked no grace; I come here in the dignity of my manhood; I have suffered the full penalty for all my mis-deeds, and now I come and demand pay for my good ones; I have a legal claim against God Almighty, and have nothing whatever to do with Jesus Christ; pay me, or I will foreclose the mortgage and take possession of the throne and all the crown jewels myself, and throw all heaven into bankruptcy. Here is a proud sinner in heaven, a single specimen of the millions sent up by the genius of the restoration fires and discipline. We will not appeal to the Bible in refutation of such doctrine, for men who can so wrest the language of the Book as to make it teach it, cannot have the least conception of its being the Word of God, or feel it to be the least authority in the settlement of any question.

Endless Misery the Most Unphilosophical and Unscriptural of all Other Theories.

The third hypothesis is that of the ever-living, conscious torments of the wicked. This, we think, is the most objectionable of all others, for by taking all its elements into the account, it not only does not admit of any kind or degree of punishment, but proposes absolute reward to every sinner, by placing him in conditions vastly superior to those he enjoys in the present life. These results grow out of the nature of its philosophy, giving every sinner an immortal soul by nature, and making the body also immortal at the resurrection. The advocates of this theory generally deny that the instrument of punishment is fire, with the exception of a very few, and even these only admit of the bare possibility of its being fire; and the explanation of the element of the torment is, that it is to the mind, what fire is to the body, and this is further defined to be remorse of conscience.

If it be literal fire, we are referred to two instances recorded in the Bible, which are supposed to prove that fire may burn continually and not consume the victims upon which it preys; but let us examine and see if even these, the only passages in all the Bible supposed to teach such an unscientific and unphilosophic idea, are indeed pertinent to the argument. One of these is the case of the burning bush Moses saw in the desert, near Mount Horeb: "And the angel of the Lord appeared unto him in a flame of fire, and in the midst of a bush; and he looked, and behold, the bush burned with fire, and the bush was not consumed. And Moses said, I will now turn aside, and see this great sight, why the bush is not burnt."—Ex. iii, 2, 3. The question is, why was not the bush consumed or burnt? We answer, because the Immortal God was in it, called the angel of the Lord, but which the whole passage shows was God himself. He restrained the action of the fire so that it could neither harm the bush or himself, and if the flame should have never ceased, still it would have been no instrument of injury to God or the bush, so let the flame and the smoke ascend up forever and ever, still immortal things or beings could not be consumed, burnt or injured, any more than though surrounded by common atmospheric air. But this is exactly the opposite fact with regard to the wicked, for God not only does not exert His power to preserve them from burning, but kindles the fires for the very purpose, and declares they shall not be restrained; but that they will consume His enemies, root and branch, reducing them to ashes and smoke.

The other instance, is that of the three Hebrew children who were cast into the fiery furnace by Nebuchadnezzar, as follows: "Then these three men were bound in their coats, their hosen, and their hats, and their other garments, and were cast into the midst of the burning, fiery furnace. Because the furnace was exceeding hot, the flame of the fire slew those men that took up Shadrach,

Meshach and Abednego. Then the king was astonished, and said unto his counsellors, did not we cast three men, bound, into the midst of the fire, and lo, I see four men, loose, walking in the midst of the fire, and they have no hurt; and the form of the fourth is like the Son of God. Then Nebuchadnezzar came near to the mouth of the burning, fiery furnace, and cried, ye servants of the most high God, come forth; and they came forth from the midst of the fire. And the king's counsellors, being gathered together, saw these men, upon whose bodies the fire had no power, nor was an hair of their head singed, neither were their coats changed, nor had the smell of fire passed on them."—Dan. iii. Here was intense fire, but it had no power to burn, or hurt these men; not even their garments; it produced not so small an effect as even to singe a hair or leave a smell of burning. The reason was, there was a Being in the flames with them, who had the power to restrain the devouring element, and render the men, and even their garments, as perfectly invulnerable in the midst of the raging flames as though it had been a cool breeze of air; and they could breathe the one as well as the other; and if the fire had continued without end, still its effect would have been the same; not a pang of pain or sensation of punishment would they have experienced to all eternity. In fact, these men, for the time being, were just as though they were immortal; perfect proof against any instrument, or agency of destruction, pain or death. Here we see that, instead of this case containing any evidence in favor of the nature of future punishment upon immortal beings, by material agents, it gives us positive argument to the contrary. Hence, the advocates of future punishment of immortal beings, by fire, need not admit even of the possibility of its being true, for it is unphilosophical to suppose that any corporial instruments can produce the least effect upon immortal nature, from which we reach the conclusion, that there is no future punishment upon this principle possible, even for a moment.

THE PUNISHMENT, A GUILTY CONSCIENCE, UNTENABLE AND ABSURD.

But it is claimed that what fire is to the material, mortal body, remorse of conscience is to the immortal mind, and *in this*, future punishment consists. If such is the fact, then it matters not where the place is, or what is the environment, or associates; and we will suppose the present world to be its theatre; and there is not, probably, a planet in all God's universe, wherein there is an equal degree of physical derangement. Now, then, we will suppose the judgment has passed, and the world remaining just as it is at present, and all the wicked, who have ever lived and died, are given this as their eternal abode.

The first impression among these men, will, perhaps, be a realization of the loss they have sustained. The righteous have a better abode, and evidently surrounded by greater sources of happiness than they have, or can ever hope to have, and for which they are conscious they have no fitness and no hope of acquiring, and understand perfectly well that their destiny is unalterably fixed, which no tears, sorrow, regret, repentance or reformation can ever change, or in the least affect. Now, would it not be the most childish nonsense to suppose these men, knowing what they now know, would sit down, and grieve and whine forever, about that which they know could never be changed? No sane man acts thus, even in the present world when he meets with losses, having so short a time to live, in which to repair the misfortune, and much less is it conceivable in a world of life and immortality which they now possess. The question now arises, what is the nature of our condition; what kind of a constitution have we, and what can we make the world, so that it will be in the greatest degree conducive to our happiness? The first fundamental fact realized, is, that they are all immortal, in both soul and body, and hence, cannot be sick, or have the least physical pain, or in the least degree be injured by other wicked men, or devils, if they had the motive or disposition to do so, knowing that no such effects can be produced upon their fellow immortals. Here is endless health, instead of almost continual suffering experienced in the world, when they were inhabitants of it before. What a glorious change is this; who would not accept it if God should make the offer now?

In the next place, there is to be no more parting with friends; death has passed away forever. We can even conceive that those who had friends in heaven would wish them back again in their own company. Another desirable bestowment, growing out of eternal life, is that there is no motive for one man to cheat another, as eternity lies equally before all, in which everything wished for may be acquired. In the passed world, it was the hurry to become rich, owing to the shortness of human life, that made men selfish and induced them to take the advantage of each other. Another troublesome element experienced in the old world, was a conscious moral responsibility to God, and a fearful apprehension of the consequences of disobedience; but this, also, has passed, and no inhabitant of the earth is ever again to be called in question by his Maker, do what he may; and to suppose such men would tantalize and torment each other mentally, would be to reduce them to the level of idiots, which another phase of the system contradicts, by declaring that they know vastly more than when in the former, temporary life.

This Hypothesis Offers Great Reward Instead of Punishment.

Their immortality also supposes that the earth will yield everything its inhabitants need. Indeed, they can have no absolute necessities; for if they did not eat they would not die, as immortal beings cannot die, and if they did not drink they could not famish, for this would suppose them mortal ; and if it would enhance their happiness, they would till the ground and cultivate the soil. O, what a beautiful world would this be made, having eternity in which to work, there would not be a spot that would not be made to bloom and blossom like the garden of paradise, every thing and condition which in any wise could be made to increase happiness and pleasure, would be done. Such is all the hell the system of a guilty conscience, philosophically admits.

Suppose now, the proposition should be made to the present sinful inhabitants of the world, of changing them into immortal beings, body as well as soul, and also to call back from the grave all their acquaintances and friends who had died, to take and to hold endless possession of the world, just as it is, would any but idiots refuse compliance? and yet, this would be voting the whole Godless human family into all the hell the remorse punishment allows. Just give man eternal life, and he is beyond the reach ef every want, every liability, every form of deprivation, or degree of suffering. Hence, eternal life is made the glorious reward of righteousness, but from which the wicked are to be forever excluded. "They shall not see life; but the wrath of God abideth on them," imprisoned already, awaiting the execution of the second death.

Here we have the various systems of future punishment, called "theology." And how can they, or any of them, appeal to the fears of any intelligent mind. Burns said:

> "The fear of hell's the hangman's whip,
> To keep the wretch in order."

But these explanations of hell, and especially those of ever-living torments, can produce no such effect upon the wretch. It is like the fabrication that at first was believed, but as the narrator began to pile up his extravagancies, all was rejected as impossible of credibility. This hypothesis of future punishment we cannot but see is in the widest contrast to that revealed in the Bible, which is so clear and palpable that it needs no explanation—no interpretation, and every attempt only serves to confuse and destroy its practical force upon the sinner. As the advocates of the endless conscious-torment theory really offer future reward to the sinner, thus holding out the glorious prize of eternal life to man, whether he remains a sinner or not, whether he serves God or satan, they should be the last to cry out against the Pagan theory of restoration, or that of no punishment at all.

The True Hypothesis Extinction of Conscious Being.

The fourth hypothesis of future punishment proposes the utter extinction of the wicked, depriving them of life and conscious existence, which carries with it every possible enjoyment, or power for evil. By the careful perusal of this little book, it cannot fail to be seen that we give no explanation, or change a single word of Scripture, or even introduce a single other rendering of a word not contained in our common version. For the last thirty years we have not heard a minister give another version of a text of Scripture, in vindication of a doctrine, than that the new idea was in direct conflict with Bible truth, found in other passages in which that particular word was not used, so that we set it down, as a rule, that the more a man changes our translation, the more error he has to promulgate. Neither have we written this book for the scholar; but in a plain, popular manner, adapted it to the common people, who always hear truth gladly, because they can understand it, while reputation and pride of opinion often masters the good sense of the popular scholar, and leads him into darkness and fatal error. Many of these very men will admit the truth of doctrines, in private conversation, but have not the moral courage to preach them in public, and we venture to remark that were the ministers of to-day to abandon their heathen dogmas of natural immortality and its long train of heresies, that there is scarcely a church membership in the country which would not follow his teaching; and if this be so, O, what a responsibility are they incurring. Many of these seem to have no misgivings in quoting the opinions of Socrates and Plato, in preference to the doctrines of Christ and Paul. Well might the Prophet exclaim, when beholding this picture in holy vision, "But they are not valiant for the truth upon the earth."—Jer. ix, 3. And also that of the Apostle Paul, "Ever learning, and never able to come to the knowledge of the truth."

The Questions Dividing the Subject, Sin and Death.

The subject of future punishment naturally divides itself into three questions. The fact of punishment, its nature, and its duration; but as we propose to discuss it, the answer to one of these questions will be seen to involve that of the others, and which is indicated in the words, "That thou shouldst destroy them which destroy the earth."—Rev. ix, 18. Here is presented the issue of the great conflict between right and wrong, truth and error, God and sin. "God made man upright, but he has sought out many inventions." God made the devil an angel of light, but he made himself a demon of darkness. The devil introduced sin into the world, and death came in consequence. "Therefore, as by one man, sin entered into the world, and death by sin; and so, death passed upon all men, for that all have sinned."—Rom. v, 12. And so the world that was made with all the elements of life and beauty, has been converted into one huge grave-yard, and its inhabitants into one long, sad, funeral procession. "Death reigned from Adam to Moses, even over them that had not sinned after the similitude of Adam's transgression."—Rom. v., 14.

Twice has God been compelled to curse the earth itself for man's sake, not in anger, or in punishment, as we conceive, but as a necessity, in order to the accomplishment of the purpose for which He made it and its inhabitants. When we use the word compelled, we wish to have it understood that we hold to the principle as a philosophic necessity, that whatever God has done in the original creation of the world and its inhabitants, and with them since, He was compelled to do, in order to accomplish His purpose, and it seems to us that any other view limits His wisdom to the standard of an experimenter, which its display in the construction of the universe most completely refutes; the destroyers, therefore, have virtually been God's opposers.

The history of the first curse is recorded in Gen. iii, 17 —20: "And unto Adam He said, because thou hast harkened unto the voice of thy wife, and hast eaten of the tree of which I commanded thee, saying, thou shalt not eat of it; cursed is the ground for thy sake; in sorrow shalt thou eat of it all the days of thy life; thorns also and thistles shall it bring forth to thee; and thou shalt eat the herb of the field; in the sweat of thy face shalt thou eat bread, till thou return unto the ground, for out of it wast thou taken, for dust thou art, and unto dust shalt thou return."

Why the World was Cursed.

The object for thus cursing the ground, was to make it a laborious habitation for man, that he might be induced the easier to seek eternal life, and a corresponding inheritance in God's new world, "The New Heaven and the New Earth." But though its soil was thus far deranged, yet was it so luxuriant and beautiful that when God sent Noah, "A preacher of righteousness," with the gospel message, to invite men to become candidates for His eternal empire, it almost utterly failed of its purpose; they turned a deaf ear to it, and acted as though they said, we have a world good enough already; our average life now is about five hundred years, and with almost perfect health; and they universally turned away from God and obliged

Him to change the order of things, or submit to a failure in obtaining loving, loyal inhabitants for His new world, the only object for which He keeps this in existence. His determination, therefore, is thus recorded: "And God saw that the wickedness of man was great in the earth, and that every imagination of the thoughts of his heart was only evil continually, and it repented the Lord that He had made man on the earth, and it grieved Him at His heart. And the Lord said, I will destroy man whom I have created, from the face of the earth; both man and beast, and the creeping thing, and the fowls of the air, for it repenteth me that I have made them."—Gen. vi, 5—7. The deluge so far destroyed the earth, in comparison with that which had existed before, that Peter speaks of it thus: "For this they willingly are ignorant of, that by the Word of God the heavens were of old, and the earth standing out of the water and in the water; whereby, the world that then was, being overflowed with water, *perished.*"—2 Pet. iii, 5, 6. It is certain that this declaration would not be true, if the present world, in its physical, surface features, bore any considerable likeness to that which had existed before. So broken and destroyed was its crust, with three-fourths of its surface covered with briny oceans, and no inconsiderable portion of the remainder, consisting of huge mountains, barren rocks, sandy deserts and myasmatic swamps, which so impregnated the air, that almost immediately after the flood the longevity of man was cut down to three score years and ten. In God's estimation, the earth was now so deranged, and the original destroyed, that He declared He would no more curse the ground, and that men would now be willing to comply with the conditions upon which an inheritance in the New Heavens and New Earth was offered, and which is demonstrated by the history of the Christian Church since. The history of the catastrophy is recorded thus: "In the six hundredth year of Noah's life, in the second month, the seventh day of the month, the same day were all the fountains of the great deep broken up (the entire crust of the earth,) and the windows of heaven were opened, and the rain fell upon the earth forty days and forty nights."—Gen. vii, 11—13. After the subsidence of the flood we have the following description and the expressed determination to which we have referred: "And Noah went forth, and his sons, and his wife, and his sons' wives with him; every beast, every creeping thing, and every fowl, and whatsoever creepeth upon the earth, after their kinds, went forth out of the ark. And Noah builded an altar unto the Lord, and took of every clean beast, and every clean fowl, and offered burnt offerings on the altar. And the Lord smelled a sweet savor; and the Lord said in His heart, I will not again curse the ground any more for man's sake; for the imagination of man's heart is evil from his youth; neither will I again smite any more everything living, as I have done; while the earth remaineth, seed time and harvest, cold and heat, summer and winter, and day and night, shall not cease."—viii, 18—22.

THE DEVIL, SINNERS, AND SIN, DOOMED TO DESTRUCTION.

Now, as the devil introduced sin into the world, and death and the curse came as a consequence, therefore he is doomed to destruction, and his judge and destroyer is to be Jesus Christ in person; for thus it is written: "For as much, then, as the children are partakers of flesh and blood, He also himself likewise took part of the same;

that through death (himself passing through death) He might destroy him that had the power of death, *that is, the devil.*"—Heb. ii, 14. That this destruction is to be accomplished at the judgment of the great day, is proved by the following Scripture: "And the angels which kept not their first estate, but left their own habitation, He hath reserved in everlasting chains under darkness unto the judgment of the great day."—Jude 6. "For if God spared not the angels that sinned, but cast them down to hell, and delivered them unto chains of darkness, to be reserved unto judgment," etc.—2 Pet. ii, 4. Here we see that the end of the devil and his angels is destruction, and if it is destruction at all, it is everlasting, eternal destruction, utter extermination, unless his Maker resurrects him again into life, which He has never promised, or threatened to do, and if He did, he would be a devil still; and that would only necessitate a second destruction; for if he is in conscious existence, his implacable will is continual hostility to the will of God, and, therefore, Christ has failed of His purpose and satan has triumphed; then "The seed of the woman has failed to bruise the serpent's head;" instead of which, he has given him the glorious boon of eternal life, which is only promised to the saints as the reward of faith and obedience. In a word, the devil lives to defy God Almighty to His face; but the silly notion is founded on the absurdity that God cannot destroy that which He has made; He is unable to unmake what He has made; a feat of which every living man and animal is capable.

Not only is the devil doomed to destruction, but his works also are to be swept out of existence, and that Christ is committed to its accomplishment is revealed thus: "He that commiteth sin is of the devil; for the devil sinneth from the beginning. For this purpose the

Son of God was manifested, that He might destroy the works of the devil."—1 John iii, 8. That the wicked are the peculiar works of the devil, indeed, his servants, his children, is shown by Christ's own words, thus: "Why do ye not understand my speech? Ye are of your father, the devil, and the lusts of your father ye will do; he was a murderer from the beginning (of the world), and abode not in the truth, (he did not continue to abide in the truth) because there is no truth in him. When he spaketh a lie, he speaketh of his own (own self); for he is a liar, and the father of it."—John viii, 43—44.

Here we see that the doom of the wicked, whom the devil has made his servants, his children, are therefore the masterpiece of his infernal work, is also that of destruction, and is to be executed by the Son of God at the judgment of the last great day; whose sentence is in these words: "Depart from Me, ye cursed, into everlasting fire, prepared for the devil and his angels.—Matt. xxv, 41. The angels of the devil are those whom he sends to do his work, whether subordinate, fallen angels, or his human children, who are led captive by satan, or his (satan's) will.

Man Lost Everlasting Life When He Sinned.

That God intended, from the beginning, to deprive sinners of everlasting life is clearly shown by the following history: "And the Lord God said, behold, the man has become as one of us, to know good and evil; and now, lest he put forth his hand, and take also of the tree of life, and eat, and live forever; therefore, the Lord God sent him forth from the Garden of Eden, to till the ground from whence he was taken. So He drove out the man;

and He placed at the east end of the Garden of Eden, cherubims and a flaming sword, which turned every way, to keep the way of the tree of life."—Gen. iii, 22—24. But notwithstanding the precaution taken by God, Adam broke through the bars, escaping the vigilance of the sleepy cherubims with their flaming sword, and plucked the immortal fruit from the tree of life, which gave him an immortal soul, and furnished him with such souls for all his posterity. They will, therefore, defeat God's plan, and still live forever in their sins; for no hell-fires or destruction can affect immortal souls. Behold, how heathen mythology is made to subvert God's great record of truth. Paul explains the everlasting punishment of the wicked, thus: "Seeing it is a righteous thing with God to recompense tribulation to them that trouble you; and to you who are troubled, rest with us, when the Lord Jesus shall be revealed from heaven with His mighty angels, in flaming fire, taking vengeance on them that know not God, and that obey not the gospel of our Lord Jesus Christ; who shall be punished with *everlasting destruction* from the presence of the Lord, and the glory of His power, when He shall come to be glorified in His saints."—2 Thess. i, 6—10. It is not common to qualify the destruction of the wicked as being everlasting, and the reason is obvious; for if destroyed at all, it must be everlasting destruction.

Destruction Always Without End.

Indeed, the destruction of anything, is everlasting destruction. A house is destroyed by fire, and it is everlasting destruction. Another house may be built upon the same site, and so much like it that no one could discover the difference, but it was not the house which was burned. This destruction of the whole man, after his resurrection, is positively declared by Christ, and refutes the foolish idea that He cannot destroy the soul because it is immortal, or supposed so to be, which if it was, of course it would be indestructable. Christ's words are these: "But rather fear Him which is able to destroy both soul and body in hell."—Matt. x, 28.

Hell, the Grave, and the Grave of Future Punishment.

This is the hell of future punishment, the lake of fire and brimstone, because it is after the wicked had come forth to damnation. Death and hell (the grave) had given up the dead which were in them, and whosoever was not found written in the Lamb's book of life was cast into the lake of fire and brimstone. This is the second death. Hell, the receptacle of the first death, had been emptied by the fiat of God, and they were judged, and now cast into the hell of fire and brimstone, the receptacle of the second death. Here death itself dies. "The last enemy that shall be destroyed, is death."—1 Cor. xv, 16. The righteous have eternal life, and the wicked have died forever, as a necessity; therefore, death is destroyed, as it hath nothing more upon which to prey. The final settlement has been made; the wicked have done the devil's work and have received his wages. "The wages of sin is death." They have sown to the flesh, and have reaped the harvest of corruption. The righteous have sown to the spirit, and of the spirit have reaped everlasting life. While the wages of sin has been death to the wicked, the gift of God has been eternal life to the righteous, through our Lord Jesus Christ. What the one class has gained, the other has lost.

"Because I have called, and ye have refused; I have stretched out my hand and no man regarded; ye have set at naught all my counsel, and would none of my reproof; I also will laugh at your calamity; I will mock when your fear cometh; when your fear cometh as desolation, and your destruction cometh as a whirlwind; when distress and anguish cometh upon you; then shall they call upon me, but I will not answer; they will seek me, but shall not find me."—Prov. i, 24—28. "He that, being often reproved, hardeneth his neck, shall suddenly be destroyed, and that without remedy."—xxix, 1. Here is the destruction again qualified. It is *without remedy*, and therefore eternal. Eternal life is the preventive, but no remedy. The idea of remedy, after destruction, is absurd.

"A fire is kindled in Mine anger, and shall burn unto the lowest hell, and shall consume the earth, and set on fire the foundations of the mountains. I will spend Mine arrows upon them, they shall be devoured with burning heat and with bitter destruction."—Deut. xxxii, 22, 24.

The Terms Describing the Punishment.

Mark the terms used to express the punishment of the wicked: "Consumed, devoured, with burning heat and bitter destruction." The Pagan theory is, that they shall be preserved forever from destruction, because they are immortal. "But the wicked shall perish, and the enemies of the Lord shall be as the fat of lambs; they shall consume;

into smoke shall they consume away."—Ps. xxxvii, 20. They are as perishable as the fat of lambs, and like it shall they consume away. Now, if a thing or being consumes, then it will come to naught, unless the consumption is arrested; but for this consumption, there is no remedy. "I will utterly consume all things from off the land, saith the Lord. I will consume man and beast; I will consume the fowls of the heaven, and the fishes of the sea, and the stumbling blocks with the wicked."—Zeph. i, 2, 3. As the heavens and the earth are to be burned up, of course the inhabitants of the sea and air are also to be destroyed.

"For as the New Heavens and the New Earth, which I will make, shall remain before me, saith the Lord, so shall your seed and your name remain. And it shall come to pass that all flesh shall come and worship before me, saith the Lord, and they shall go forth, and look upon the carcasses of the men that have transgressed against me; for their worm shall not die, neither shall their fire be quenched; and they shall be an abhorring unto all flesh." —Isa. lxvi, 22, 24.

The Place where the Wicked were Consumed an Eternal Monument.

It will be observed that this is the "hell-fire" in which the wicked have been consumed, and nothing but carcasses left. It will also be seen that the place was in the New Heavens and New Earth which is to be made. From this and other parallel passages we propose to introduce, it will be seen that this spot where the wicked had been extinguished, is to remain a standing monument forever of God's indignation against sin. The saints are to go forth and look upon the carcasses of the transgressors, and be reminded of the dread effects of opposition to the will of God, and we do not consider it unlikely, or an unnecessary precaution to take, in order to prevent a repetition of the experiment of the first Adam. It was not the soul, the living being, that had been cast into hell-fire, that thus remained, for these had been consumed to mere dead carcasses, and we see by other passages, that they had been reduced by fires, beyond the carcasses, to mere dead ashes and smoke. The fires and worms of decomposition had not been arrested, and had therefore accomplished the work of utter destruction. This was in accordance with the original decree, "Of dust thou art, and unto dust shalt thou return." It is not declared, or even implied, that the fires had not gone out of their own accord, when they had spent their fury upon the wicked, nor that the worms of corruption had not destroyed the living body; indeed, these were reduced to carcasses; and how could the worms be immortal, and the fires eternal, when the men upon whom they had preyed were reduced to nothing but fleshless carcasses? And if a man is reduced to a carcass, he is beyond the further reach of suffering, and should the worms continue to live, and the fires to burn, there would be no further torment to the dead carcass. The only idea taught in this language, so often repeated both in the Old and New Testaments, is, that when God kindles fires, or lets loose other instruments of destruction, no power can arrest their ravages until the work is complete; it is, therefore, " Everlasting fire," perfect consumption, and the result, eternal destruction, " Punished with everlasting destruction."—Paul.

Wicked Men and Devils are to be Punished on the Earth.

There is not the least intimation in all the Bible, that the wicked, either men or devils, are to be taken from the earth to receive judgment or punishment; on the contrary, the Judge and punisher is to come to the earth for that purpose. "Lo, I come, and My reward is with Me, and My work before Me." "Then shall He reward every man according to his works, whether they be good or bad."

The Location of Hell.

The hell of the wicked, the lake of fire and brimstone, to be prepared for the devil and his angels (his servants,) is to be on the earth, and its locality is not only fixed, but revealed in the Bible, just as definitely as that of Jerusalem. The following is a part of the evidence upon this subject: "And he (king Josiah) defiled (destroyed) Tophet, which is in the valley of the children of Hinnom, that no man might make his son or his daughter to pass through the valley to Molech." The valley of the son of Hinnom was in the land of Edom, south of Jerusalem. —2 Kings xxiii, 10. The fact that here the idolatrous Jews, mixing with the heathen, kept continual fires burning, and consumed human beings as sacrifices, making it a place of human slaughter, so much resembling hell, was the reason why God selected it, and used it to impress upon the mind an approximate conception of what hell will be and its fires do. This was only the type, and of small dimension; but we shall see that it will be enlarged to meet the necessities, and that its name is changed from Tophet to a Place of Slaughter. We may remark that it will not take a place as large as one-fourth of the State of New York to hold all the wicked of the earth; we mean all those who are, or will be, candidates for this destruction; for we have elsewhere shown that it is limited to those who have had the light of the gospel, and persistently and finally rejected its salvation, its offer of eternal life. "And they have built the high places of Tophet, which is in the valley of the son of Hinnom, to burn their sons and their daughters in the fire, which I commanded them not, neither came it into My heart; therefore, behold, the days come, saith the Lord, that it shall no more be called Tophet, nor the valley of the son of Hinnom, but the valley of Slaughter; for they shall bury in Tophet till there is no place, and the carcasses of this people shall be meat for the fowls of the heaven, and for the beasts of the earth; and none shall fray them away."—Jer. vii, 31—33.

"Behold, the Lord cometh from far, burning with anger, and the burden thereof is heavy; His lips are full of indignation, and His tongue as a devouring fire, and His breath as an overflowing stream, shall reach to the midst of the neck, and the Lord shall cause His glorious voice to be heard, and shall show the lighting down of His arm, with the indignation of His anger and with the flame of a devouring fire, with scattering tempest, and hailstones; for Tophet is ordained of old; yea, for the king it is prepared; the pile thereof is fire and much wood, and the breath of the Lord, like a stream of brimstone, doth kindle it."—Isa. xxx, 27, 28, 30, 33. Here, hell is to be made; its fires kindled by the breath of God like a stream of brimstone, and it is in the day when He cometh in His indignation; consequently, it does not now exist. It is prepared for the king, as well as the lowest of the wicked, and the punishment is to be upon the earth. "And it shall come to pass in that day, that the Lord shall punish the host of the high ones that are on high, and the kings of the earth upon the earth."—Isa. xxiv, 21.

"Come near, ye nations; and hearken, ye people; let the earth hear, and all that is therein; the world, and all things that come forth of it, (here God issues a universal proclamation, setting forth His determination with the wicked; well will it be for those who take timely heed) for the indignation of the Lord is upon all nations, and His fury upon all their armies; (now the Prophet sees what will be the end, and continues,) He hath utterly destroyed them; He hath delivered them to the slaughter; (it will be remembered that Tophet was to be called a *place of slaughter*) their slain also shall be cast out, and their stink shall come up out of their carcasses, and the mountains shall be melted with their blood. (It will add intensity to the fires.) And all the host of heaven shall be dissolved, and the heavens shall be rolled together as a scroll, and all the host shall fall down, as the leaf falleth off from the vine, or as a falling fig from the fig-tree; (this shows that it is the last great day of the world's dissolution,) for My sword shall be bathed in heaven; behold, it shall come down upon the land of Idumea, (the Greek name for Edom, in which is the valley of the son of Hinnom,) and upon the people of My curse, to judgment. The sword of the Lord is filled with blood; it is made fat with fatness, and with the blood of lambs and goats, with the fat of the kidneys of rams; (this consumption of the wicked was typified by burning the beasts in sacrifice after they were slaughtered, and here is the antitype,) for the Lord hath a great sacrifice in Bozrah, (the capitol of Edom, as we see by chapter lxi, 1,) and a great slaughter in the land of Idumea; and the unicorns shall come down with them, and the bullocks with the bulls; and their land shall be soaked with blood, and their dust made fat with fatness; for it is the day of the Lord's vengeance, and the year of recompenses for the controversy of Zion; and the streams thereof shall be turned into pitch, and the dust thereof into brimstone, and the land thereof shall become burning pitch; (nothing is easier than for God to change the gases of the dust and stones into brimstone, and "His breath like a stream of brimstone is to kindle it,") it shall not be quenched night nor day; (no power shall interfere to put out the fires and rescue the victims alive,) the smoke thereof shall go up forever; (as long as there is a vestige of a human being or devil to burn.) From generation to generation it shall lie waste; none shall pass through it forever and ever, (The fires, however, have gone out, as the description which is here given clearly proves,) but the Cormorant and the Bittern shall possess it; the Owl also and the Raven shall dwell in it; (how could the birds dwell in it if the fires had not gone out?) and He shall stretch out upon it the line of confusion, and the stones of emptiness. They shall call the nobles to the kingdom, but none shall be there, and all her princes shall be *nothing*. (They were put there; now mark, they are *nothing*. If this does not express utter destruction, then words are without meaning.) And thorns shall come up in her palaces, nettles and brambles in the fortresses thereof; and it shall be an habitation of dragons, and a court for owls; the wild beasts of the desert shall also meet with the wild beasts of the island, and the Satyr shall cry to his fellow; the Screech Owl also shall rest there, and find for herself a place of rest; there shall the Great Owl make her nest, and lay, and hatch, and gather under her shadow; there shall the vultures also be gathered, every one with her mate. Seek ye out of the Book of the Lord, and read, no one of these shall fail."—Isa. xxxiv.

THE QUENCHLESS FIRES GO OUT.

It is easy to see that no word could more conclusively prove that the quenchless fires, and God's instruments of corruption and destruction had ceased with the existence of the wicked, than this representation of plants and animals, reproducing from generation to generation, upon the very spot where the lake of fire and brimstone had once consumed the wicked. Isaiah has another vision of the Great Christ, the destroyer of the destroyers, after He had accomplished the work of exterminating the devil and his work, in the land of Edom, the great valley of slaughter, as follows: "Who is this that cometh from Edom, with dyed garments from Bozrah; this that is glorious in his apparel, traveling in the greatness of his strength? (Then comes the answer.) I that speaketh in righteousness, mighty to save. (If He is mighty to save His saints, which takes place at the same time, He is also mighty to destroy His enemies.) Wherefore art thou red in thine apparel, and thy garments like him that treadeth in the wine-fat? I have trodden the wine-press alone, and of the people there was none with Me, (it is Christ's work *alone*, to destroy the devil and his works) for I will tread them in mine anger, and trample them in My fury; and their blood shall be sprinkled upon My garments, and I will stain all My raiment;

for the day of vengeance is in mine heart, and the year of My redeemed is come. And I looked, and there was none to help; and I wondered that there was none to uphold; therefore, mine own arm brought salvation unto Me, and my fury it upheld Me. And I will tread down the people in mine anger, and make them drink in My fury, and I will bring down their strength to the earth."—Isa. lxiii, 1—6. Such a scene as this does not depend upon any particular word, the meaning of which might be doubtful, as to the certainty and duration of the punishment of the wicked; but the whole representation is one of absolute slaughter; it is the slaughter of men, not spirits, including the wicked of all time. "He that soweth to the flesh shall of the flesh reap corruption." They had been called from their graves, just as they had died, "to shame and everlasting contempt." They have had their resurrection to damnation. While the righteous dead have been raised to incorruption, the wicked have reaped the opposite harvest. "For whatsoever a man soweth, that shall he also reap; be not deceived; God is not mocked; for he that soweth to his flesh, shall of the flesh reap corruption; but he that soweth to the spirit, shall of the spirit reap life everlasting."—Gal. vi, 7, 8.

The Great Contest Between Christ and the Wicked at the Last Day.

This scene declared to the Prophet was also shown by Christ to the Revelator, and so connected with the great harvest, gathered by the angels at His command, with the concurrent events at the end of the world, that leaves no possibility of honest misunderstanding. "And I saw heaven opened; and behold, a white horse; and

He that sat upon him was called Faithful and True, and in righteousness He doth judge and make war. His eyes were as a flame of fire, and on His head were many crowns; and He had a name written, that no man knew but He himself; and He was clothed with a vesture dipped in blood, and His name is called the Word of God. (This is recorded in the first of John's gospel, "In the beginning was the Word, and the Word was with God, and the Word was God." So we see that this *Word* of God was God himself.) And the armies which were in heaven followed Him upon white horses, clothed in fine linen, white and clean; and out of His mouth goeth a sharp sword, that with it He should smite the nations; and He shall rule them with a rod of iron; and He treadeth the wine-press of the fierceness and wrath of Almighty God; and He hath on His vesture, and on His thigh, a name written, King of kings, and Lord of lords. And I saw an angel standing in the sun, and he cried with a loud voice, saying to all the fowls that fly in the midst of heaven, come and gather yourselves together unto the supper of the Great God, that ye may eat the flesh of kings, and the flesh of captains, and the flesh of mighty men; and the flesh of horses, and them that sit on them; and the flesh of men, both free and bond, both small and great. (The birds of prey feast upon the slaughtered dead; the worms riot in the flesh of the mighty, until the fires of God are kindled, which consumes all to ashes and smoke.) And I saw the beast, and the kings of the earth, and their armies, gathered together, to make war against Him that sat upon the horse, and against His army; and the beast was taken, and with him the false prophet that wrought miracles before him, with which he deceived them that had received the mark of the beast, and them that worshiped his image. These both were cast alive into a lake of fire, burning with brimstone; and the remnant were slain with the sword of Him that sat upon the horse, which sword proceeded out of His mouth; and all the fowls were filled with their flesh."—Rev. xix, 11—21. "And I looked; and behold, a white cloud; upon the cloud one sat like unto the Son of Man, having on His head a golden crown, and in His hand a sharp sickle; and another came out of the temple, crying with a loud voice to Him that sat on the cloud, thrust in thy sharp sickle and reap, for the time is come for thee to reap, for the harvest of the earth is ripe. And He that sat on the cloud thrust in His sickle on the earth, and the earth was reaped. And another angel came out of the temple, which is in heaven, he also having a sharp sickle. And another came out from the altar, which had power over fire; and he cried with a loud cry to him that had the sharp sickle, saying, thrust in thy sharp sickle and gather the clusters of the vine of the earth, for her grapes are fully ripe; and the angel thrust in his sickle into the earth, and gathered the vine of the earth, and cast it into the great wine-press of the wrath of God; and the wine-press was trodden without the city, and blood came out of the wine-press even unto the horse-bridles, by the space of a thousand and six hundred furlongs,"—Chapter xiv, 14—20.

Here is a great slaughter-yard, in which God has decreed to slay His enemies. Behold the dreadful carnage, and after which, to kindle it into a vast lake of fire and brimstone, and consume them all to ashes. Its dimensions, as here given, is two hundred square miles. The valley of the son of Hinnom was thus enlarged, according to the prediction of Isaiah. Into this great wine-press of the wrath of God the wicked, "The vine of the earth," around which their heart's affections had entwined, are gathered into clusters, bound in bundles by the harvest angels, cast into it and burned. If any sentimental skeptic or moralizing rejector of the Word of God dissents from such suffering or slaughter of human beings, as being inconsistent with the character of God, we refer him to the history of the human species, for an answer. Behold, the two hundred and sixteen billions of mankind who have lived and died, half of them in perfect innocence, in all the forms of agony and suffering to which it is possible to subject men. Now, if God has thus subjected the life of the world, for the accomplishment of His revealed purpose, to the painful suffering of one death, why not a fourth of these to a second death, for the same reason? And that these, too, are the most guilty of all, having had and rejected the offer of eternal life, why cannot God cause these to live again and be thus disposed of, so that they would not escape with only the suffering of the first death, shared equally by the most innocent inhabitants of the world? Surely, what has been, may be again.

The Infliction of the "Second Death."

The infliction of this death, the place of its execution, and the instruments to be employed, are presented again by the Revelator, thus: "And I saw a great white throne, and Him that sat on it, from whose face the earth and the heaven fled away; and there was found no place for them. And I saw the dead, small and great, stand before God; and the books were opened; and another book was opened, which is the Book of Life; and the dead were judged out of those things which were written in the books, according to their works. And the sea gave up the dead which were in it; and death and hell delivered up the dead which were in them; and they were judged, every man according to their works; and death and hell (contents of the grave) were cast into the lake of fire. This is the second death, and whosoever was not found written in the book of life, was cast into the lake of fire." —Rev. xx, 11—15.

Here closes the conflict between right and wrong for ever; every sinner, whether man or devil, is dead: death itself is extinct, having no more life upon which to prey. God, the only source of immortality, has conferred the hallowed boon upon the saints, and they live for ever. Death has ceased to reign. Satanic dominion is no more, and the victims of his cruel hate, though his willing subjects, have shared the same common fate; Christ has triumphed and the reign of immortality begun.

This subject, Christ presented in a parable to the disciples, and here we give His own interpretation, and which will be seen to be in perfect corroboration of, and harmony with, the description of Isaiah and the Revelator. "Then Jesus sent the multitude away, and went into the house; and His disciples came unto Him, saying, declare unto us the parable of the tares of the field. He answered and said unto them, he that sowed the good seed is the Son of Man; the field is the world; the good seed are the children of the kingdom, but the tares are the children of the wicked one; the enemy that sowed them, is the devil; the harvest, is the end of the world, and the reapers are the angels. As, therefore, the tares are gathered and burned in the fire, so shall it be in the end of this world. The Son of Man shall send forth His angels, and they shall gather out of His kingdom all things that offend, and them which do iniquity, and shall cast them into a furnace of fire; there shall be wailing and gnashing of teeth. Then shall the righteous shine forth as the sun, in the kingdom of their Father. Who hath ears to hear, let him hear."— Matt. xiii, 36—43.

Surely, such an interpretation needs no other to make it understood, and we only desire to call attention to a figure, Christ here employs, to show that the wicked are consumed, burnt up: "As, therefore, the tares are gathered and burned in the fire, *so* shall the wicked be gathered in the end of this world, and burned." It is repeated in the 49th and 50th verses, thus: "So shall it be at the end of this world; the angels shall come forth, and sever the wicked from among the just, and shall cast them into the furnace of fire; there shall be weeping and gnashing of teeth." Here is Christ's plain teaching, and to the effect, that, just as the noxious, vegetable tares are burned up in a furnace of fire by the husbandman, so will the wicked be cast into a furnace of fire and burned up at the end of this world, and the wailing and gnashing of teeth consequent upon the burning will last as long as conscious existence, and no longer.

WICKED WRESTING OF THE SCRIPTURES.

The only way to make out the opposite theory, is to say, Christ, I do not believe your teaching, for I hold to the heathen doctrine that the soul is immortal, and after the resurrection, the body will be immortal also; and, therefore, it cannot be burned or consumed; I propose, therefore, to change the language of your parable, and interpret your interpretation so as to make it suit Plato's immortal-soulism. Hence, I say that the fire in which men gather and burn tares, is figurative fire, that is, no fire at all; and the tares are not burned, but preserved forever and ever, and you should have understood the use of language better than to have made such a representation; at least, you should have given another edition of your Book, so that it would harmonize with our dear Plato. O Christ, how have they fouled thy Word with their feet.

Scripture Testimony that the Wicked will be Destroyed.

We have seen that the instrument God uses in executing this punishment, is called "A flame of devouring fire." Plato, however, says he is immortal, and cannot, therefore, be devoured. Who is to be believed, God or Plato? The wicked are here represented as having been first slain, and then burned till they became "*nothing*," but the lying vanities of heathen mythology says, the soul is immortal, and, therefore, it cannot become "nothing;" and modern theology takes sides with the mythology, and, of course, against the Book of God. "But the wicked shall perish, and the enemies of the Lord, as the fat of lambs they shall consume; into smoke shall they consume away."—Ps. xxxiv, 20. What language can express extinction of being more perfectly than this? And it leaves the Platonists no alternative but flat denial, as an immortal thing cannot consume at all, much less into smoke, or the gases of which man is known to be composed. "Let the sinners be consumed out of the earth, and let the wicked be no more."—Ps. civ, 35. David was a prophet, and here is an inspired prayer; will it be answered? "For evil doers shall be cut off; but those that wait upon the Lord, they shall inherit the earth (New Earth;) for yet a little while, and the wicked shall not be; yea, thou shalt diligently consider his place, and it shall not be."—Ps. xxxvii, 9, 10. What disposition will the heathens make of these words. They will be obliged to call in Origen, and he will tell them that the words of the Bible must never be taken to convey any sensible ideas; these must be found in mysterious allegory; and in this passage, would mean quite the contrary, and should have been translated, "Evil doers live forevermore;" and the reason for this rendering of the passage, is, that Plato says the soul is immortal, and the holy Catholic Church has ever believed him, and the holy Catholic Church is infallible. "For the day of the Lord is near upon all the heathen, they shall be as though they had not been."—Obad. 15, 16. Here is God's testimony by another concurring prophet. Now, how can ever-living, conscious torment be reconciled with it? What say the disciples of Socrates to such doctrine? "And now, also the axe is laid unto the root of the trees; therefore, every tree which bringeth not forth good fruit, is hewn down, and cast into the fire. Whose fan is in His hand, and He will thoroughly purge His floor, and gather His wheat into the garner; but He will burn up the chaff with unquenchable fire."—Matt. iii, 10, 12. Here the wicked are no more than chaff, before God's quenchless fires; and again, the heathen theory is in direct antagonism, for its immortals, instead of being as highly combustable as chaff, are perfect salamanders. "The sinners in Zion are afraid; fearfulness hath surprised the hypocrites. Who among us shall dwell with devouring fire? Who among us shall dwell with everlasting burnings?"—Isa. xxxiii, 14. Here the hypocrites are becoming alarmed at teaching heathen doctrines in opposition to Christianity, and beginning to seriously ask the question, whether, after all, it is possible to dwell with everlasting burnings and not be devoured; and we have no doubt but that the controversy upon this subject, now so widely spreading, will lead thousands to abandon Plato and embrace Christ. "For the Lord God of hosts shall make a consumption, even determined in the midst of all the land, for yet a little while, and the indignation shall cease, and Mine anger in their destruction."—Isa. x, 23, 25. Now, if God's indignation can only be satisfied with the ever-living punishment of the wicked, then His indignation will never cease, for they will never be destroyed. Here again, the teachings of God and Plato are at variance: which shall we receive? "He that believeth on the Son, hath everlasting life; and he that believeth not the Son, shall not see life; but the wrath of God abideth on him."—John iii, 36. Here is a living unbeliever, and his destiny is, that he shall not see life. Now, this must mean the temporary resurrection-life of the wicked, in order to appear before the judgment-seat of Christ, and to end with the second death, or it means eternal life. But the instruction of the whole Bible upon this subject is, that eternal life is promised to the righteous, and that the wicked are to be raised to temporary life; hence, it is the everlasting life which the unbelievers shall not see.

"And if thy hand offend thee, cut it off; it is better for thee to enter into life maimed, than having two hands to go into hell, into the fire that never shall be quenched; where their worm dieth not, and the fire is not quenched."—Mark ix, 45, 46. As we have before remarked, it must be observed that it is not that the fire is not to go out, after having consumed to ashes that upon which it preys; but until then, it cannot be arrested in its ravages; for to quench, is, to put out so that the thing burning is not consumed. In regard to the expression, "Their worm dieth not," it is evident that the same idea is intended to be conveyed. These are the worms that nature uses to decompose all animal bodies, as Job says: "Though worms destroy this body, yet in my flesh shall I see God." In his immortal resurrection-body, in contrast to the corrupt resurrection bodies of the wicked. If it is true that the worms prey upon the wicked in hell, then they draw their life from them, and are nourished, and grow upon the substance of the wicked, who, of course, are devoured in the same degree or ratio; consequently, there must come a time when they will cease to suffer, because they will cease to be, and the worms will no more die until this is accomplished, than they do in the coffins of the dead at present, until all is consumed but the bones; as they do die now and will die then, for the want of food; besides, how can the worms live in hell fires? Now, unless the worms do thus decompose the wicked in hell, they not only cannot die, but they cannot begin to live; for it is the prior decomposition of nature that produces the conditions upon which the worms come into life; that is, they must first die before they can decompose; then the atmosphere commences its work of transformation, and when putridity is reached, the worms come into life and finish the work of destruction. As the wicked are just as corrupt then as when they died, the work of destruction will be just as rapid as now; for it is not to be arrested by the interference of God, in killing the worms and granting respites, for their worm shall not die.

"THE WORM SHALL NOT DIE."

The necessities, therefore, in the case, are that the worms will consume the corrupt wicked (for corruption is the harvest they have reaped) in hell, in just as short a space of time as they do the dead now lying upon the surface of the earth, and exposed to the decomposing ravages of the atmosphere. The work of the worms also presupposes that the wicked are already dead, and very far advanced in putrescence, as it is only in this condition that the worm begins to live. These are not only the philosophic necessities in the case, but they are the exact conditions revealed in the Bible of the manner of the punishment of the wicked. They are first gathered from off all the earth by the angels, and cast into a place called hell. They are then and there slaughtered by Jesus Christ in person, or by the angels at His order. The worms and birds of prey now do their natural work. This is succeeded by the kindling of the whole land where the wicked are gathered, into a vast lake of fire and brimstone. "The breath of the Lord like a stream of brimstone doth kindle it."—Isa. This reduces all to smoke and ashes, and the wicked are "punished (as Paul says) with everlasting destruction," not preservation.

The following passage is supposed to contain similar evidence for the endless continuance of the conscious suffering of the wicked; but we shall see that it is a mere sophisticated torturing of the Words of God, just like all others, to make them teach Platonic philosophy: "And the third angel followed them, saying, with a loud voice, if any man worship the beast and his image, and receive his mark in his forehead, or in his hand, the same shall drink of the wine of the wrath of God, which is poured out without mixture, into the cup of his indignation; and he shall be tormented with fire and brimstone in the presence of the holy angels, and in the presence of the Lamb; and the smoke of their torment ascendeth up forever and ever."—Rev. xiv, 9—11. "And to you who are troubled, rest with us, when the Lord Jesus shall be revealed from heaven, with His mighty angels, in flaming fire, taking vengeance on them that know not God, and that obey not the gospel of our Lord Jesus Christ, who shall be punished with everlasting destruction from the presence of the Lord."—2 Thess., 7—9.

It will be observed that in one of these passages, the torment is to be inflicted by the Lamb, and *in His presence*, and in the other, the destruction is to be *from His presence*. It is *in His presence* while the wicked live and suffer, and *from His presence* when they are destroyed or cease to exist. You stand and see a mansion take fire; the firemen make every effort to quench the fire, but without avail; you watch it until it is consumed to ashes and smoke; it is now destroyed from your presence, and it is also destroyed from God's presence, as it does not exist; but it could not be destroyed from your presence or from His presence if it was not consumed, or did not cease to exist. The house also perished, by unquenchable fire, as it could not be put out. The expression "The smoke of the wicked ascended up forever and ever," conveys the same idea as "Their worm dieth not," and we suppose, the very reason why they were used, was to show that the wicked were to be consumed, devoured, and not kept in endless, living torments, as in the Tartarian dens of the heathen, where immortal souls never cease to be tortured.

"The Smoke of Their Torment" goes out.

Smoke is the result of decomposition or consumption, and necessitates the extinction of the things or beings from which it ascends. Mark the expression, it is not the smoke of the brimstone, or other fuel, but the smoke of *their torment*, of *their consumption*. It is "*their worm*," and not any outside instrument of torture that gnaws, and that never dies; therefore, there is no smoke arises from the wicked if they do not consume; and if it does arise, they do consume, and into ashes and smoke; and when they are thus consumed, the smoke must cease to rise, and the worm cease to gnaw, for the want of fuel or substance. The expression, therefore, forever and ever, is limited to the time of burning and gnawing.

The Meaning of the Words Forever and Ever not Necessarily Endless.

The meaning of the words forever, and forever and ever, are relative, whether used in the Bible or in any other book, or intelligently spoken, and that in the Scriptures especially. They are constantly applied to things which have an end. And as the wicked are mortal, and never to have eternal or everlasting life, or immortality, therefore, no terms applied to their existence or suffering, means endless, for if they have no existence they cannot suffer endless misery. In proof of this, we quote the following passages: "Then his master shall bring him unto the Judges; he shall also bring him unto the door-post; and his master shall bore his ear through with an awl;

and he shall serve him *forever.*"—Ex. xx, 6. That is, as long as the man lives. Hence, "forever" is not endless. "And if he be not redeemed within the space of a full year, then the house that is in the walled city shall be established forever, thoughout his generations. It shall not go out in the jubilee."—Lev. xxv, 30. Here the word "forever" is not endless. "All the heave offerings of the holy things, which the children of Israel offer unto the Lord, have I given thee by a statute *forever* before the Lord; but the Levites shall do the service of the tabernacle forever throughout your generations."--Num. xviii, 19, 23. Here the word forever, was limited to the existence of the Jewish tabernacle, and does not mean endless. "Then shall there enter into the gates of this city, kings and princes, sitting upon the throne of David, riding in chariots and horses, they and their princes, the men of Judea, and the inhabitants of Jerusalem; and this city shall remain forever." (but the city was burned up.)—Jer. xvii, 25. "But if ye will not hearken unto Me to hallow the Sabbath day, and not to bear a burden, even entering into the gates of Jerusalem on the Sabbath day; then I will kindle a fire in the gates thereof, and it shall devour the palaces of Jerusalem, and it shall not be quenched." —Jer. xvii, 27. Here are the words "forever" and unquenchable fire defined, and both limited to the existence of the Jewish dynasty and the City of Jerusalem. This destruction took place in accordance with a prediction of Christ, and by Titus, a Roman General, A. D., 70. It is brought out by the parable of a King, who made a marriage for His Son, meaning God and Christ: "But when the King heard thereof (how the Jews treated the servants who were sent to invite them to the marriage) He was wroth; and He sent forth His armies, and destroyed those murderers, and burned up their city."—Matt. xxii, 7. The destruction of Jerusalem was everlasting destruction, as a Jewish dynasty, and the fires which consumed it were "unquenchable;" God kindled them for the purpose, and they could not be put out or quenched, but they went out of their own accord when the consumption of the city and the murderers, was complete. So, if we let the Author of the Bible explain His own terms, by the use He makes of them, all is easy and natural, while the opposite course is that which He denounces thus: "Every day they wrest My words, all their thoughts are against Me for evil."—Ps. lvi, 5. "Seeing we have received this ministry, we have renounced the hidden things of dishonesty; not walking in craftiness, nor handling the Word of God deceitfully, but, by the manifestation of the truth, commending ourselves to every man's conscience in the sight of God."—1 Cor. iv, 1, 2. "Even as our beloved brother Paul, also, according to the wisdom given unto him, hath written unto you, in all his epistles, speaking in them of these things, (the burning of the heavens and the earth, and the ungodly, in the last day. Read the whole chapter.) in which are some things hard to be understood, which they that are unlearned and unstable, wrest, as they do also the other Scriptures, unto their own destruction."—2 Pet. iii, 15, 16. It is plain to see that those who wrest the Scriptures are unlearned in them, and their only study of them is to make them appear to teach their creeds and preconceived doctrines, thus: "Teaching for doctrines, the commandments of men." They may be learned in the theological literature of men, and even that of received science and philosophy, but the estimation God puts upon that, is this: "For the wisdom of the world is foolishness with God; He taketh the wise in their own craftiness, and the Lord knoweth the thoughts of the wise, that they are vain; therefore, let no man glory in men."—1 Cor. iii, 19 —21. "For the foolishness of God, is wiser than men." "But we preach Christ crucified, unto the Jews a stumbling-block, and unto the Greeks, foolishness." Here were the wise Greeks, who certainly understood their own Greek language better than any modern Greek scholars, yet to them the gospel was "foolishness." Just so the gospel of Christ's real death and resurrection, and that of His saints, upon which their future conscious existence depends, as well as the destruction of the wicked, is foolishness to these learned Greek scholars. Now, the great mass of the Greeks, to whom Paul preached Jesus and the resurrection, and immortality depending upon the resurrection, refused His doctrine, calling it foolishness, and Paul himself, "a babbler," (See Acts xvii,) and preferred the wise teachings of their own Grecian philosophers, Socrates and Plato, who believed in the natural immortality of the soul, and that the soul is the living, thinking, feeling inhabitant of the body, out of which it moves at what is called, but which is not death, only a separation of the living inhabitant from a lifeless house. Thus do they wrest the Words of God, to make them appear to teach the doctrines of Socrates and Plato, and cover the iniquity of thus rejecting Christ and the resurrection, the only source and manner of immortality to man, by vain attempts to make the Greek language teach Platonic theology, instead of Christ's gospel.

This Discussion a Subject of Prophesy, Connected with the Coming of Christ.

Never before in the history of the world have the professed ministry of the gospel devoted themselves, privately and publicly, to this work, as at the present time, and it would be wonderful, if such an event, of so much importance to Christ's true Church, (His saints) had not been made a subject of prophetic prediction. That God saw it and inspired it to be written, is recorded in various places in His Word, one picture of which is the following: "I charge thee, therefore, before God and the Lord Jesus Christ, who shall judge the quick and the dead at His appearing and His kingdom; preach the Word (not your words, but Mine); be instant in season and out of season; reprove, rebuke, exhort with all long suffering and doctrine; for the time will come when they will not endure sound doctrine, but after their own lusts they shall heap to themselves teachers, having itching ears; and they shall turn away their ears from the truth, and shall be turned unto fables."—2 Tim. iv. In the preceding chapter he gives us another part of the picture, thus: "This know also, that in the last days, perilous times shall come, (then he gives a description of the various sins of which those will be guilty who have a form of Godliness, and by which acts they deny the power; which, if any man will read, and take all those guilty of such things out of the present professed Christian Church, he will not find many left. Paul then goes on and gives the character of the teachers of this people): "Ever learning and never able to come to the knowledge of the truth." Then follows a picture of the Spiritualists, who also resist the truth; men of corrupt minds, reprobate concerning the faith. "Now, as Jannes and Jambres withstood Moses, so do these always resist the truth. But they shall proceed no further; for their folly shall be manifested unto all men, as theirs also was." The folly of Pharaoh and his army was found out when they were destroyed in the Red Sea, in listening to the familiar Spiritualists. This was the peril to which they were thus exposed. And in the days of these false religious teachers, and these magicians, Jesus Christ shall come in the clouds of heaven, with power and great glory, and to reward those who have not been ashamed of His words, and destroy them who have wrested them. Hence, "In the last days, perilous times shall come."

LIMITATION OF THE WORDS EVERLASTING.

The covenant of circumcision was everlasting, and yet Christ abolished it. "Then will I cause you to dwell in this place, in the land that I gave to your fathers, *forever and ever.*"—Jer. vii, 7. The Jews, however, have been dispossessed of that land, and by God's intervention, most two thousand years; and if they had complied with the conditions of possession, still it would have shared in the general conflagration of the world; hence, the words forever and ever are limited to the duration of the thing or being to which they are applied, which duration must be ascertained from other sources of information. "They said, turn ye again now, every one of you from his evil way, and from the evil of your doings, and dwell in the land that the Lord hath given unto you, and to your fathers, forever and ever."—Jer. xxv, 5. This was the land of Canaan, and if the words forever and ever, meant without end, then the promise has failed, for the Turks have owned and dwelt in that land for more than twelve hundred years. These were the terms of the old covenant, God made with Abraham, and which the new covenant abolished, and the words forever and ever were limited to the existence of the old covenant. We have seen that the wicked, being mortal, which existence is opposite to that of the righteous, who are to be immortal, (not mortal) will die, and this is the reward awaiting them. "The wages of sin is death," "They shall not see life;" therefore, the words forever, and forever and ever, are limited to their existence. If it is the everlasting God, it means without beginning or end. If it is the everlasting Gospel, it means the duration of the present world, with which it ceases to exist. If it is the everlasting kingdom of God, it means without end, from the time it is set up in the New Heavens and New Earth. If it is Christ, a priest forever, it is limited to the dispensation of mercy to mankind. If it is that Christ ever liveth to make intercession for the saints, it ends with the work of mediation, and that with the existence of the present world. If it is the everlasting hills, they are to end with the world also. If it is the joys of the saints at God's right hand, in His kingdom, which are forevermore, they have no end. If it is the everlasting wailings of the damned, they cease with the existence of the wicked. If it is eternal judgment, it means only the duration of the judgment at the last day, the end of which is already described. If it is the everlasting fires of hell, they go out with the consumption of the wicked, which reduces them to ashes and smoke. If it is the smoke of their torment ascending up forever and ever, it ceases when there is nothing more of the wicked to burn or smoke. Hence, the words everlasting, forever, forever and ever, or even eternal, of themselves, do not express endless duration, or that the things which they describe are without end.

The Words "Vengeance of Eternal Fire," not Endless Misery.

That the mistake in supposing the opposite, may not honestly be made, God has furnished us with an example, thus: "Even as Sodom and Gomorrah, and the cities about them, in like manner, giving themselves over to fornication, and going after strange flesh, are set forth for an example, suffering the vengeance of eternal fire."—Jude 7. The short history of this destruction, is as follows: "The sun was risen upon the earth when Lot entered into Zoar. Then the Lord rained upon Sodom and Gomorrah, brimstone and fire from the Lord, out of heaven; and He overthrew those cities, and all the plain, and all the inhabitants of the cities, and that which grew upon the ground. And Abraham got up early in the morning to the place where he stood before the Lord; (that was on the previous day, while he pleaded for the city of Lot, his nephew,) and he looked toward Sodom and Gomorrah, and toward all the land of the plain; and behold, and lo, the smoke of the country went up as the smoke of a furnace; and God destroyed the cities of the plain."—Gen. xix, 23—25, 27—30.

This conflagration was in 1898, B.C., since which time there is the Dead Sea covering the spot where the cities stood. The quenchless, eternal fires went out just as soon as the people and their dwellings ceased to exist, at least, after having consumed the soil and the earth deep down, making the bed for the sea of death. Mark the expression; it is the vengeance of eternal fire. It is eternal vengeance. The very suffering is eternal, in the language, yet they did not consciously suffer a single hour, or no longer than a man could suffer in a rain of fire and brimstone, and we suppose God added the brimstone in mercy, which suffocated, with a few inhalations, every living thing, before the fires consumed them. Thus, if God is permitted to explain His own terms, there is no room left for the ever-living, conscious torments of heathen philosophy. We add one passage more, and leave the Bible view of the subject: "Behold, the day cometh that shall burn as an oven; and all the proud, yea, and all that do wickedly, shall be stubble, (not immortal beings,) and the day that cometh shall burn them up, saith the Lord of hosts, that it shall leave them neither root nor branch. (How much is left of a plant, if its roots and branches, every one of them, are burned up?) But unto you that fear My name shall the sun of righteousness arise, with healing in His wings; (giving them eternal life, where there shall be no more sickness and no more pain,) and ye shall go forth, and grow up as calves of the stall; and ye shall tread down the wicked, (know ye not that the saints shall judge angels?) for they shall be ashes under the soles of your feet, in the day that I shall do this, saith the Lord of hosts."—Mall. iv, 1, 2. Here is the destiny of all the proud and wicked of the world, "Punished with everlasting destruction."

A Three-Fold Argument.

In relation to the nature and duration of this punishment, and which show the destruction of the wicked is to come to an end, and not to be continuous, we introduce three passages which qualify each other:

First.—" Depart from Me, ye cursed, into everlasting fire, prepared for the devil and his angels; and these shall go away into everlasting punishment, but the righteous into life eternal."—Matt. xxv, 46.

That the punishment is everlasting destruction, and not preservation, is proved by the second passage, thus: " Who shall be *punished with everlasting destruction* from the presence of the Lord and the glory of His power."—2 Thess., i, 9.

" But rather fear Him, which is able to destroy both soul and body in hell."—Matt. x, 28.

Third.—" Thou hast rebuked the heathen, thou hast destroyed the wicked, thou hast put out their name forever and ever; O, thou enemy! *destructions are come to a perpetual end;* their memorial is perished with them."—Ps. ix, 5, 6.

Look at this three-fold argument: First.—It is everlasting punishment. Second.—The punishment, is everlasting destruction. Third.—The *destruction comes to a perpetual end.* Is it possible for infinite wisdom to construct an argument more conclusive than this against the heathen doctrine of " endless misery "?

Origin of the Doctrine of Endless Torments, Heathen Philosophy.

That we may have a proper view of the origin and nature of the doctrine of the immortality of the wicked and of endless torments, we introduce those of Socrates and Plato, his pupil, who, by universal consent, are acknowledged to be the best authority and exponents of heathen mythology. "And now the Author of all things thus addressed the geni, to whom He had confided the government of the stars; Ye gods, who owe to Me your birth, listen to My sovereign commands. You have not a title to immortality, but you may partake in it by power of My will, more potent than the bonds which unite the parts of which you are composed, to fill with inhabitants the sea, the earth, and the air. Were these creatures to receive life from me, they would be exempt from the empire of death, and become equal to the gods themselves; I, therefore, commit to you the care of producing them. Delegates of any power, unite to perishable bodies the germs of immortality, which you shall receive from me, and form those beings who have command over other animals, to remain subject to you. Let them receive birth at your command, live to increase by your benefactions, and after death, let them unite to you and share in your happiness. He said, and immediately pouring into the cup in which he had mixed the soul of the world, the remains of what he had reserved of that soul, he composed the souls of individual creatures, adding to those of man, a portion of divine essence, and annexed to them irrevocable destinies.

"Then it was decreed that mortals should be born, capable of knowing and serving the divinity; that the man should have the pre-eminence over the woman; that justice should consist in triumphing over the passions, and injustice in yielding to them; that the just, after death, should pass into the stars, and there enjoy unalterable felicity; and that the unjust should be changed into women, or if they continued unjust, transmigrated into different animals; and that they should not be restored to their primitive dignity until they should become obedient to the voice of reason. After these immutable decrees, the Supreme Being disseminated souls into the different planets, and commanded the inferior gods to clothe them successively with mortal bodies, to provide for their wants and to govern them. He then entered again into eternal repose. The immortal and rational soul was assigned its place in the brain, the most elevated part of the body, to regulate its motions."—Plato. "Selections of a Father," pages 170, 171.

Socrates on the Immortality of the Soul.

My friends, there is still one thing which is very just to believe; if the soul be immortal, it requires to be cultivated with attention, not only for what we call the time of life, but for that which is to follow; I mean eternity; and the least neglect here, may be attended with endless consequences. If death were the final dissolution of being, the wicked would be great gainers by it, by being delivered at once from their bodies, their souls and their vices; but as the soul is immortal, it has no other means of being freed from its evils, nor any safety in them, but in becoming very good and very wise; for it carries nothing away with it but its good or bad deeds, which are commonly the consequences of its education, and the cause of eternal happiness or misery.

When the dead are arrived at the rendezvous of departed souls, whither their demon conducts them, they are all judged. Those who have passed their lives in a manner neither entirely criminal nor absolutely innocent, are sent into a place where they suffer pains proportioned to their faults, till being purged and cleansed of their guilt, are afterward restored to liberty, and receive the reward of their good actions done in the body. Those who are judged to be incurable on account of the greatness of their crimes, who have deliberately committed sacrileges or murders, and other such offences, the fatal destiny that passes judgment upon them hurls them into Tartarus, from whence they never depart. But those who are found guilty of crimes great indeed, but worthy of pardon, who have committed violence in the transports of rage against their father or mother, or have killed some one in a like emotion, and afterwards repented, these suffer the same punishment, and in the same place, but, for a time only, till, by their prayers and supplications, they have obtained pardon from those whom they have injured. But those who have passed through life with peculiar sanctity of manners, delivered from their earthly abodes as from a prison, are received on high, in a pure region, which they inhabit; and, as philosophy has sufficiently purefied them, they live without their bodies through all eternity, in a series of joys and delights it is not easy to describe, and which the shortness of my time will not permit me to explain more at large.

"What I have said, will suffice, I conceive, to prove that we ought to endeavor strenuously, throughout our whole lives, to acquire virtue and wisdom, for you see how great a reward, and how high a hope it proposes to us. And though the immortality of the soul were dubious, every wise man ought to assure himself that it is well worth his trouble to risk his belief of it, in this manner; and, indeed, can there be a more glorious hazard? We ought to enchant ourselves with this blessed hope, for which reason I have lengthened this discourse so much."
—"Selections of a Father," pages 234—236.

SOCRATES WENT TO HEAVEN AT DEATH.

Goldsmith says: "Socrates employed the last day of his life in entertaining his friends upon this great and important subject, from which conversation, Plato's admirable dialogue, entitled "The Phedon," is wholly taken. He explains to his friends, all the arguments for believing the soul immortal, and refutes all the objections against it, which are very nearly the same as are made at this day. When Socrates had done speaking, Crito asked him: 'In what manner he thought fit to be buried?' As you please, said Socrates, if you can lay hold of me, and I not escape out of your hands. At the same time, looking at his friends with a smile, said: 'I can never persuade Crito, that Socrates is he who converses with you, and disposes the several parts of his discourse, for he always imagines that I am what he is going to see dead in a little while; he confounds me with my carcass, and therefore asks me how I would be interred.'"—"Goldsmith's History of Greece," page 185.

Here is the heathen doctrine of the future state of rewards and punishments, and we have already seen that not a single element of it is taught in the Bible.

HOW THE HEATHEN DOCTRINE OF ENDLESS MISERY CAME INTO THE CHURCH.

It was principally introduced into the so-called Christian Church, (but which, in fact, brought the Papal Church into existence,) by Origen, a Platonic philosopher, though a Presbyter of Antioch. Dr. Mosheim says, "The principles which gave rise to another species of theology, and which was called 'Mystic,' was derived from the same source as the scholastic. The authors of this mystic science are not known, but the principles from which it sprung, are manifest. Its first promoters proceed from that well-known doctrine of the Platonic school, which was also adopted by Origen and his disciples, that the divine nature was diffused through all human souls; that the faculty of reason, from which proceeds the health and vigor of the mind, was an emanation from God, and comprehended in it, all truth, human and divine." It is easy to see that if this opinion is true, there is no further use of a Revelation, or of a Bible, for whatever it teaches is to be submitted to human reason, wherein resides all truth, human and divine, for its decision. Hence, we have the decision of the holy fathers, prominent among whom was Origen, and that decision comprehends the infallible dogmas of the Romish Church: hence, also, the hatred of that Church to the Bible, and the positive dread of its free circulation. The historian continues: "Origen entertained the notion that it was extremely difficult, if not impossible, to defend the Bible, so long as it was explained according to the real import of its terms. He, therefore, had recourse to the fecundity of a lively imagination, adopting that maxim of theirs which asserted the innocence of defending the truth by artifice and falsehood; and maintained that the Holy Scriptures were to be interpreted in the same allegorical manner that the Platonists used in explaining the history of the gods. In consequence of this pernicious rule of interpretation, he alleged that the words in the Scriptures, were, in many places, void or sense; and though in others there were, indeed, certain notions conveyed under the outward terms, according to their literal form and import, yet it was not in these that the true meaning of the sacred writers was to be sought, but in a mysterious sense arising from the nature of things themselves. This hidden sense he endeavors to investigate throughout his commentaries, neglecting and despising for the most part, the outward letter.

In this devious path he displays the most ingenious strokes of fancy, and always at the expense of truth, whose divine simplicity is scarcely discernable through the cobweb vail of allegory. Nor did the inventions of Origen end here, for he divided this hidden sense, which he pursued with eagerness, into moral and mystical, or spiritual. The moral sense of Scripture displays those doctrines that relate to the inward state of the soul and conduct of life. The mystical sense represents the nature, laws, and history of the world; and we have not yet reached the end of the labyrinth, for he sub-divided this mystical world of his own creation into two distinct regions, one of which he called the superior heavens, and the other, the inferior, by which he meant the Church. This led to another division of the mystical sense into an allegorical, or earthly one, adapted to the inferior world, and an anagogical, or celestial sense, adapted to the superior region. Thus were the doctrines of Christ fatally corrupted by the prince of darkness, coming as an angel of light, in the person of a Presbyter, but still nothing but a heathen philosopher, and only making a profession of Christianity because Constantine had made it the religion of the empire in the place of his Platonic Paganism.

CATHOLICISM FOUNDED ON HEATHENISM.

Here and thus was laid the foundation of the Papal Church, upon Plato, and not Peter, and much less upon Christ. Now, with such a foundation, what better superstructure could be erected thereon, than that of the Great Mystic Babylon of the Bible, the mother of harlots, and abominations of the earth, whose exhaustless fountain of corruption has infected the whole moral, mental, civil and religious world.

The historian continues: "Origen was the great model whom the most eminent Christian doctors followed, in their explanation of the truths of the Gospel, and which were consequently explained according to the rules of the Platonic philosophy, as it was corrected and modified by this learned father. Those who desire a more ample and accurate account of this matter, may consult Gregory Nazianzen, Platonist among the Greeks, and Augustine, among the Latins, who for a long time were followed as the only patterns worthy of imitation, and who, next to Origen, may be considered the parents and supporters of the philosophical, or scholastic theology, and who were both zealous Platonists, holding for certain all the tenets of that philosophy, which were not totally repugnant to the truths of Christianity; (what those were, may be gathered from the fact that he still held to the transmigration of human souls into cats,) these were laid down as fundamental principles, and they drew from them a great variety of subtle conclusions, which neither Christ nor Plato ever thought of."—"Mosheim's Ecclesiastical History," vol. 1, page 276.

Our readers may now be able to trace these doctrines of a future state, back through the holy fathers of Roman Catholicism, directly to the heathen mythology of Socrates, and Plato, his pupil, who, after he had learned all his master could teach him, as he was now dead, went to Egypt to perfect his education. Egypt, in those days, was the most renowned school of the world. It must also be remembered that the doctrines of Origen, Plato and Socrates, originated with the Pagan priests of Egypt. See "Platonic Theology," by Prof. Lewis.

We do not like to draw comparisons between Jesus Christ and a man, but as Socrates is considered the father of this heathen, moral philosophy, and the best exponent of the mythological future state after death, and the manner of escape into it, which he was just going to experience, let us hear what the founder of Christianity had to say about His approaching death and survival from it.

SOCRATES DID NOT DIE, HE ONLY MOVED OUT OF HIS BODY; BUT JESUS DID DIE.

"Jesus said unto them, the Son of Man shall be betrayed into the hands of men; and they shall kill Him, and the third day He shall be raised again."—Matt. xvii, 22, 23. Socrates was not going to be killed, he was only going to separate from his body, or carcass. "And the angel answered and said unto the women, fear not, for I know that ye seek Jesus, which was crucified; He is not here, for He is risen, as He said. Come, see the place where the *Lord lay*."—Matt. xxviii, 5, 6.

Here we see that the Lord himself had laid in the grave, but Socrates had not; he had escaped and ascended up to heaven; nothing but his carcass was in the grave.

Jesus, however, did not ascend to heaven until forty days afterward, and then He took His carcass with Him. While the soul of Socrates was immortal, and did not die, the soul of Jesus was mortal, and died, and was in the grave.

"Thou wilt not leave My soul in hell, (the grave, for He "descended into the lower parts of the earth,") neither wilt thou suffer thine Holy One to see corruption." Here was also the Holy One, in the grave. "Men and brethren, let me freely speak unto you of the patriarch David, that he was both dead and buried, (though Socrates was not,) and his sepulcher is with us unto this day; therefore, being a prophet, and knowing that God had sworn with an oath to him, that He would raise up Christ to sit on his throne; he seeing this before, spake of the resurrection of Christ; that His soul was not left in hell, neither did His flesh see corruption. This Jesus hath God raised up, whereof we are all witnesses." David has not ascended into the heavens, but Socrates has.

That Christ was changed from mortality to immortality, by His resurrection from the dead, we have such proof as this: "If the spirit of Him that raised up Christ from the dead, dwell in you, He that raised up Jesus from the dead shall also quicken your mortal bodies by His spirit that dwelleth in you."—Rom. viii, 2. Hence, Christ had no immortal soul, if Socrates had, and Christ only went to heaven through the resurrection, while Socrates went without any resurrection; his immortality was natural endowment. Not only so, but the manner in which God makes the immortal saints or souls such, is perfectly evident from such Scripture as this: "If Christ be not risen from the dead, then they that have fallen asleep in Christ are perished." If their Lord had remained dead and perished, so had His saints. "I am the way, the truth, and the light. I am the resurrection and the life." Out of Christ, therefore, there is no life of any kind, or degree, in the future; and none in Him, but to the saints, and it comes only through the same resurrection the Lord himself passed.

The Doctrine of Immortality by Christ in the Resurrection Fatal to Romanism.

If there was equal evidence in the Bible for the heathen view of going to heaven at death, and natural immortality, (but for which there is not a particle,) as there is for the resurrection of life, and immortality, and no heaven till that event, which would leave the preachers of the Gospel equally free to preach the latter, and had they pursued this course as they did in the apostolic age, with the exception of a few heretics, who overthrew the faith of some, by preaching that the resurrection passes on every man when he dies; we say, had this been done, the Roman Catholic Church would never have existed, as it is perfectly incompatable with these truths. Instead of Peter, with his keys, sitting in heaven, opening and shutting its gates, for the admission of Catholics and the rejection of Protestants, he lies asleep in his grave, and in the very day he died " his thoughts perished ;" he, therefore, knows nothing of the mystical operation. Instead of the Virgin Mary being in heaven, hearing Papish prayers, and interceding her hard-hearted Son in their behalf, she perished when she died, and will remain thus, as did her Great Son, until the resurrection rescued Him. Hence, she knows nothing of her idol worshipers.

Instead of the infernal indulgence of purgatory, which offers certain salvation, by the merit of its fires, to all Catholics, at the contempt of Christ and His merits, the foolish prayers are stripped of the mystic shrines, and if they should call as loud as did the priests of Baal, still the dead, cold ears of the "Canonized" would be heedless to the cries. Just dismiss Socrates, Plato and Origen, with their natural immortalism, and preach Jesus and the resurrection, and Oh, what multitudes of the deluded would embrace the gospel and be saved. In a word, take heathenism out of Papacy, and all the depths of satanic art could not keep it alive.

Not only so, but what an illumination from God's Great Bible would inundate the religious world. How the absurdities, that the dead are alive, that they have gone into heaven instead of the grave, that Abel, though he has been in heaven six thousand years, is to be brought out, and judged "whether he is good or bad." Cain, who committed the first murder, has been burning in hell's torments for six thousand years, still, he is to have a short respite, under a divine habeus corpus, and tried, to ascertain whether he is guilty. Besides, he has suffered six thousand years longer in hell than it is possible for the last murderer to suffer; and inflicted, too, by a just God.

Socrates saw that it would be gross injustice for his heathen gods to administer such awards, and he, therefore, invented Purgatory, to get them out, after they had become sufficiently purified by the purgatorial fires. Jesus Christ declared, "No man hath ascended up into heaven at any time," but Socrates declared that all the virtuous go immediately to heaven when they die. Whose testimony is true? Who is to be believed? And yet, people calling themselves Christians, turn away their ears from these great truths of Christ and the Gospel, and cling to those here shown to belong to Pagan idolatry. If we have any hesitancy in choosing between these opinions of heathens and Papists, on the one side, and the truths taught by Jesus Christ on the other, for fear of losing popularity, it will be well to reflect upon such warnings as these: "Whosoever is ashamed of Me and of *My Words*, of him will I be ashamed before My Father and His holy angels." —Mark viii, 38. "And whatsoever is made known as secret, that publish upon the house-top."—Jesus.

The Origin of Purgatory.

Here originated the doctrine of purgatory. The practice of praying sinners out of it; the immortality of the soul; the ever-living torments of the damned; that death is not death, but a separation; that the body is nothing but a carcass, a prison-house, a tenement for the soul, which is the man proper, the thinking, feeling, living, immortal inhabitant; that at death, the good go immediately into heaven, and the wicked into hell; that the salvation depends upon the performance of good works, and the damnation upon bad ones, the one merits heaven and the other hell; that bodiless spirits live, think, and feel, and the wicked are hurled into Tartarus, or Hades, where Pluto presides. Some of the tortures practiced in these dens, are described substantially as follows: "Some of the sufferers are imprisoned in pools of water, which, by continual pumping, can be kept from submerging them; but they become exhausted, then the water rises above their heads, when they endure all the pains of suffocating and strangulation, yet they cannot die, as they are immortal, and the ceaseless monotony only alternates between exhaustion and the death struggles of drowning men. Another mode of torment is, that the victims are starving with hunger, and before their eyes, is a table furnished with the choicest fruits and meats calculated to enhance the appetite, but the length of their chain is too short to enable them to reach the wished-for repast, and they are thus doomed to suffer the famishing sensation of hunger, without a moments alleviation, to all eternity. Others are chained to pillars, with their hands bound, amid wild vultures, which forever prey upon their vitals, gnawing the heart, liver, and lungs, but which, by a law of the gods, were reproduced, so that the pain of being eaten alive was experienced, without the least respite. No instrument could destroy these beings, or put them out of existence; even the gods that made them could never unmake, for the immortal soul was a part of the gods themselves."

Heathen Future Punishment Adopted by Protestantism.

To show how completely the fictitious fables of this heathen Tantalus have been adopted by the Christian Church, we quote the following poetic description from the pen of a minister:

> "Fast by the side of this unsightly thing
> Another was portrayed, more hideous still,
> Who sees it once, shall wish to see it no more;
> Forever undescribed let it remain!
> Only this much I may or can unfold,
> Far out it thrust a dart that might have made
> The knees of terror quake, and on it hung,
> Within the triple barbs, a being, pierced
> Through soul and body. Of heavenly make,

Original, the being seemed ; but fallen,
And worn, and wasted with enormous woe ;
And still, around the everlasting lance,
It writhed, convulsed, and uttered mimic groans ;
And tried and wished, and ever tried and wished
To die, but could not die. Oh, horrid sight !
I, trembling, gazed and listened, and heard this
Voice approach my ear: 'This is eternal death.'
Nor these alone. Upon this wall,
In horrible emblazonry, were lined
All shapes, all forms, all modes of wretchedness
And agony, and grief, and desperate woe ;
And prominent in characters of fire,
Where 'er the eye could light, these words you
Read : 'Who comes this way, behold, and fear to sin.'
Amazed, I stood and thought such imagery
Fortokened, within, a dangerous abode ;
But yet, to see the worst a wish arose,
For Virtue, by the holy seal of God
Accredited and stamped, immortal all,
And all invulnerable, fears no hurt.
As easy as my wish, as rapidly, I
Through the horrid rampart passed, unscathed
And unopposed ; and, poised on steady wing,
I hovering, gazed. Eternal justice ! sons
Of God ! tell me, if ye can tell, what then
I saw, what then I heard. Wide was the place,
And deep as wide, and ruinous as deep ;
Beneath, I saw a lake of burning fire,
With tempest tost perpetually, and still
The waves of fiery darkness 'gainst the rocks
Of dark damnation broke, and music made
Of melancholy sort ; and over head,
And all around, wind warred with wind,
Storm howled to storm, lightning, forked lightning
Crossed, and thunder answered thunder, muttering
Sounds of sullen wrath. As far as sight
Could pierce, or down descend in caves of
Hopeless depth, through all that dungeon

Of unfading fire, I saw most miserable
Beings walk, burning continually, yet
Unconsumed ; forever wasting, yet enduring
Still ; dying perpetually, yet never dead.
Some wandered lonely in the desert flames,
And some in full encounter fiercely met,
With curses loud, and blasphemies, that made
The cheek of darkness pale ; and as they fought,
And cursed, and gnashed their teeth, and
Wished to die, their hollow eyes did utter streams
Of woe. And there were groans that ended not,
And sighs that always sighed, and tears that
Ever wept, and ever fell, but not in mercy's
Sight. Sorrow, repentance and despair,
Among them walked, and to their thirsty lips
Presented frequent cups of burning gall.
And as I listened, I heard these beings curse
Almighty God, and curse the Lamb, and curse
The earth, the resurrection morn ; and seek,
And ever vainly seek, for utter death ;
And to their everlasting anguish still,
The thunders from above, responding, spoke
These words, which through the caverns of
Perdition forlornly echoing, fell on every ear:
' Ye knew your duty, but ye did it not.' "
—"*Pollock's Course of Time,*" *pages 36—40.*

THE HERESY OF EXALTING SATAN TO BE CHRIST'S COMPEER.

Here is satan exalted to be a most despotic king, whom Christ was committed to destroy, but failed. Sinners, his prominent work, instead of being destroyed, are made immortal, despite His power. In the great contest, Omnipotence fled, vanquished, from the field; death, the devil, the wicked, live forever, and sin is eternal, reigning over half of the human species, although thus it is written: "Afterward, they that are Christ's at His coming, then cometh the end, when He (Christ) shall have delivered up the kingdom to God, even the Father, when He shall have put down all rule, and all authority and power; for He must reign, till He hath put all enemies under His feet. The last enemy that shall be destroyed is death."—1 Cor. xv, 24—26. It is clear from this, that the putting all His enemies under His feet, is destroying them. But here the haters of Christ are exalted to eternal power and immortal authority, ruling without end. Behold! through the infernal heathen mythology, how the Son of God has failed of His declared purposes, and the devil is triumphant. Behold the damnable heresy, in the last degree, insulting and degrading to Christ and His Gospel. See how the teaching of heathen priests is preferred to Christ's Great Gospel. Listen no more to the voice amid the horrid din of discord of Plato, and let Jesus be silent; cry out no more, "Give us our Barrabas, and let Jesus be crucified." Thus, by a touch of the heathen mythological wand of interpretation, destruction means eternal preservation; death means eternal life; and the Good God of the Bible is confounded with the monster Molech.

Eternal Misery Forbids the Possibility of Loving God.

God teaches man to love his enemies; to do good to them who hate, and despitefully use and persecute him; but behold! how He hates His enemies. Behold! how malignantly He pursues them, not willing to burn them up, which might easily be reconciled with justice, and even with mercy, they having refused to answer the purpose of their being; but to keep them alive in order to torment them, when, if He would take off His hand, they would die in a few moments by the raging flames of fire and brimstone. Behold your mother, father, sister, brother, wife, husband, child, writhing in the ceaseless flames of hell, and you are in the kingdon of God. Ten thousand years have passed away, and you see your child, only daughter, boil up to the surface in the fiery cauldron, lifting her sorrowful eyes, inquires, "How long, O Lord; how long?" God responds, "Eternally, eternally, eternally." She casts a horrid glance toward the mother and God, and swings off into another ten thousand, at the end of which time the lake of fire makes another circle; looking more blackened, scorched, haggard and ghastly, and with hollow eyes, uttering streams of woe, sees her mother again, whose only happiness has been to gaze down among the damned, to catch a glimpse of her own dear daughter; now hearing the same cry, "How long, O Lord; how long?" but only to hear the wretched, wrathful response, "Misery without end, misery without end." How much do you think that mother can enjoy heaven?

But, it is said, God so changes the nature of the saints that they will feel happy at seeing their friends thus suffer. Great God, what a statement! to change the nature of the saints into the most perfect conception of demons, who are supposed to enjoy the sufferings of others. Their minds are to be so far belittled, nay, destroyed, that they will understand injustice to be justice; resentment, mercy; hatred, love; and the infliction of misery, kindness. Their nature will be so hardened that it will be unmoved to pity, at the deepest anguish—worse than the most debased monster that ever trod the earth of sin. The conversion is to be such that the saints will love God and hate their own friends, so as not to feel a pang of suffering at their most excruciating anguish. In a word, God once loved His enemies, and commanded His people to do so also; but He has changed himself, and has miraculously changed His saints, so that all can hate their enemies together. Behold, what an infernal scheme of lying philosophy is here invented to corrupt the doctrines of Christ's great love and justice toward man.

But there is another and more dreadful aspect of these heathen doctrines even than this. This charges God with requiring impossibilities of His people. He has implanted in man's nature, a principle which compels him to hate a tyrant. Now, the doctrine of endless misery converts God into an omnipotent tyrant, and therefore renders it impossible for a man to love Him. Let us suppose a man appears at the judgment for examination, and some such questions as the following, are put to him: "Did you ever love Me while in the world which has now ended; and were you not moved to fear Me because of My endless-misery doctrine?" "Yes; but I thought it would not be so bad with the wicked after all, and I would find this out when I came here." "Well, now you have seen how I have proceeded against the sinner, and that they are now in the lake of fire and brimstone, and how I keep them alive, and intend to do so, world without end." "Yes; I have seen my child cast into it, and now behold him writhing and wishing to die, but cannot, as you keep him alive on purpose to prolong his conscious misery; and I have learned that you will not be satisfied unless it continues endlessly; and ever since I learned your real determination, which I hoped might be otherwise, I have suffered and must suffer to all eternity, and it would be a great relief for me to die." "Well, do you love Me now, and will you serve Me?" "I will serve you; I will do anything for you which I have the power to do; but I do not love you, and I cannot. When I was in the world I always hated a tyrant, and I never saw one who would make others suffer for his mere gratification, which only resulted from the execution of his ambitious schemes; but you make these poor creatures suffer for your own pleasurable glory, or selfish honor. Indeed, I was tortured even to see a dog kept alive to prolong his suffering, and my nature led me to relieve its torments by putting it out of conscious existence. Because I dread your punishment, I will not only do anything of which I am capable to avoid its infliction—I will even profess to love you; but as you have made me to hate tyrants, and you are an omnipotent one, I cannot love you; and if you admit me, and every man has these same feelings in regard to tyrants, then you must have your kingdom inhabited by slaves of fear, and if you will only admit subjects who profess to love you, then it will be filled with hypocrites as well; but if you only admit those who really love you, and as that is impossible, you will never have any subjects at all, and all must go to hell together."

This is the God of endless misery; and it is the God of heathen mythology as well. In vain does the Good God of the Bible protest against associating Him with these. While this is the disposition of the gods, from whom even Socrates says, "It was never supposed came virtue," listen while the living God speaks upon this subject: "As I live, saith the Lord God, I have no pleasure in the death of the wicked. Turn ye, turn ye, for why will ye die." Yes, the heathen priests of endless misery reply, you do have pleasure in the death of the sinner, and you keep him always dying, whereas, if you had no pleasure in his death, you would let him die at once. Therefore, this theology makes God swear to a lie, making Him gratified and glorified at the endless misery of sinners. But what care the heathen doctors for the Words of God? Plato is their expounder of Scripture. Give us our own dear Plato; he can tell us what God means; him will we hear in all things.

God's Ministers and Plato's.

God makes one effort more to convince the ministers of heathenism of the truths of Christianity. Oh! that they would hear. "For God so loved the world that He gave His only begotten Son, that whosoever believeth in Him, should not perish, but have everlasting life." But Plato stirs up his ministers, and they come again with their deceitful handling of the Word of God, and respond to this passage, "Yes; but the word perish, means not to perish, but to be preserved from perishing." They cannot perish, for then they would escape endless misery, and our own, wise Dr. Plato says the soul is the man, and the soul is immortal; the word perish, therefore, should have been translated, imperishable, and this is what the Greek word requires; so God, you must permit us to point out the errors in your Book. The passage should have read: "You so loved the world that the gift of your Son did not prevent men from perishing," for they were immortal through Adam, and having eternal life, they could not receive it as a gift from your Son, and it is a pity you had not read Socrates, and the Greek scholar, Plato, before you sacrificed your Son, and you would not have made such a mistake.

How will such contemners and dispisers of God's Words appear, when the time described as follows, arrives? "He that is ashamed of Me and of My Words before a perverse generation, of him will I be ashamed before My Father and the holy angels."

Eternal Life Offered to the Righteous.

Another argument of our hypothesis is, that eternal life is offered as a reward to the faithful, and to be conferred in the resurrection at the last day. The promise is made in such language as this: "Be thou faithful unto death, and I will give thee a crown of life."—Rev. ii, 10. The crown of life is the symbol of victory over death and the grave, and, therefore, is eternal life. This was said to encourage the martyrs, so that if they did fall victims to the first death, and that in its most terrible forms, yet they should have, by the confirment of eternal life, the victory over the second death. The instruction to them was, that if they fulfilled the conditions of faithfulness until death, losing their lives for Christ's sake, He would see to it that they should receive the crown of life, which would forever render them triumphant over all the power of death and the grave, and is thus indicated: "So when this corruptable shall have put on incorruption, and this mortal shall have put on immortality, then shall be brought to pass the saying that is written; death is swallowed up in victory; O death, where is thy sting? O grave, where is thy victory?"—1 Cor. xv, 54, 55.

If there was nothing more said in the Bible, as to the time when the crown of life was to be awarded, except this verse, it might be inferred that it was at death, but even this would be a very strange procedure, to encourage a man to do that for which he would be killed; but when he came to the killing, instead of receiving the crown of life, he was disappointed, and received the chain of death. All, however, that is here stated, is, that if faithful unto death, I will give the crown of life when the time comes, according to My plan and proposition for its bestowal. You have died in the possession of My spiritual nature, and by which you are sealed with My promise of eternal life. That this is the truth, we quote as follows: "In whom ye also trusted, after that ye heard the word of truth, the gospel of your salvation; in whom also, after that ye believed, ye were sealed with that holy spirit of promise, which is the earnest (the spirit of it, that which is enjoyed in anticipation) of our inheritance, until the redemption of the purchased possession."—Eph. i, 13. To show further that it is the spiritual assimilation of man to Christ, the "partaking of the divine nature," which is the condition of his resurrection to eternal life, we also quote the following: "For if the spirit of Him that raised up Jesus from the dead, dwell in you, He that raised up Christ from the dead shall also quicken your mortal bodies by *His spirit that dwelleth in you.*"—Rom. viii, 11.

In order to settle the question as to the time when eternal life, or immortality, which is the same thing, is to be given, or to show what the teachings of the Scriptures upon the subject are, we introduce the following somewhat extended testimony, as it is one of those questions upon which there is a great deal of honest difference of opinion, and very much confusion; indeed, it is of such importance, that the view which confers eternal life upon man, either at birth or death, renders a resurrection of the dead impossible; for if Christ's life or soul, or it matters not what it is called, did not die, then it was not brought back to life; because, as nothing but life can die, and as nothing but that which died can be raised from the dead, therefore, if Christ did not die, He did not rise from the dead. Hence, if the Pagan philosophy is true, that Christ's soul was always immortal, and therefore could not die, then it sweeps away the whole foundation of the Christian system, and gives as a substitute the doctrine of the Nicolaitanes, which declared that Christ only died in appearance, and rose in appearance, which thing it is no marvel God declares, "I hate."

Heathenism Knew Nothing of the Immortality of the Gospel.

Heathenism knew nothing about the immortality Paul preached, but it was brought to light by the Gospel; and now we introduce more extensively the Gospel of immortality, "Who will render to every man according to his deeds. To them who by patient continuance in welldoing, seek for glory, and honor, and immortality, eternal life."—Rom. ii, 6, 7. Here it is positively shown that Paul did not have immortality, or eternal life, but according to the promise of God, was patiently waiting for it. If then, Paul did not have immortality and eternal life, in the present life, has any other Christian got these? Much less, do the wicked possess them? Again the same Apostle says, "I am now ready to be offered, and the time of my departure is at hand. (His martyrdom was approaching.) I have fought a good fight; I have finished my course; I have kept the faith; henceforth, there is laid up for me a crown of righteousness, which the Lord, the righteous judge, shall give me at that day; and not to me only, but to all them that love His appearing."—2 Tim. vi, 7, 8. Paul was one of those in the Church of Smyrna, to whom it was said, "Be thou faithful unto death and I will give thee a crown of life;" but he knew he was not to receive it until the day of judgment, and then the saints of all ages are also to receive them at once.

No Rewards or Punishments till the Resurrection at the Last Day.

"Set your affections on things above, and not on things on earth; for ye are dead, (ye Christians are dead, and have not eternal life,) and your life is hid with Christ in God; when Christ, who is our life, shall appear, then shall ye also appear with Him in glory."—Col. iii, 3. This patient seeking of the saints for glory, honor, immortality and eternal life is also presented in the following forcible language: "For our light afflictions, which are but for a moment, worketh for us a far more exceeding and eternal weight of glory, while we look not at the things which are seen, but at those things which are not seen; for things which are seen are temporal; but the things which are not seen are eternal." He then contrasts these temporal and eternal things under the figures of a transcient tabernacle and an eternal house, the one signifying our present mortal being, and the eternal, immortality with which the saints are to be clothed, or into which they are to be resurrected, or if alive upon the earth at that time, suddenly changed. "For we know that if our earthly house of this tabernacle were dissolved, we have a building of God, an house not made with hands, eternal in the heavens, (New Heavens.) For in this we groan, earnestly desiring to be clothed upon with our house which is from heaven; if so be, that being clothed, we shall not be found naked. For we that are in this tabernacle do groan, being burdened; not that we would be unclothed, (he did not desire to die,) but clothed upon, that mortality might be swallowed up of life. Now, He that hath wrought us for the self-same thing, is God, who also hath given unto us the earnest of the spirit; therefore, we are always confident, knowing that, whilst we are at home in the body, (this mortal body,) we are absent from the Lord, (absent from the Lord in the immortal body.) For we walk by faith, and not by sight, (while we look and wait for the eternal things;) we are confident, I say, and willing rather to be absent from the body, (the mortal body in which we now groan,) and to be present with the Lord, (when the Lord comes with His crown, and when mortality shall be swallowed up of life,) wherefore we labor, that whether present or absent, we may be accepted of Him; for we must all appear before the judgment-seat of Christ, that every one may receive the things done in his body, according to that he hath done, whether it be good or bad."—2 Cor. iv, 17, 18, and v, 1—10.

From such teaching, nothing can be more clear than that Paul had no immortality, or eternal life—had no crown or reward, and did not expect any, until received at the judgment-seat of Christ. He also said, " God shall be magnified in my body, whether it be by life or death; for me to live, is Christ, and to die, is gain. I am in a strait betwixt two, having a desire to depart and to be with Christ, which is far better." But we have seen that he did not expect to be with Christ until the judgment, nor to receive his crown, till that event. He further discourses, thus: "But I would not have you to be ignorant, brethren, concerning them which are asleep, that ye sorrow not as others, which have no hope, for if we believe that Jesus died and rose again, even so them also which sleep in Jesus will God bring with Him; for this we say unto you by the Word of the Lord, (it is God's recorded truth,) that we which are alive and remain unto the coming of the Lord, shall not prevent them which are asleep, for the Lord himself shall descend from heaven with a shout, with the voice of the archangel, and with the trump of God; and the dead in Christ shall rise first; then we which are alive and remain, shall be caught up together with them in the clouds, to meet the Lord in the air; and so shall we ever be with the Lord; wherefore, comfort one another with these words."

THE SAINTS NOT TO BE WITH THE LORD UNTIL HE COMES AGAIN.

The saints are now to be forever with the Lord, but not forever in the clouds; but only till the world is dissolved by the fires of the last day, and re-created into the New Heavens and the New Earth; after which, as we have said, John saw the Lord himself, and all His saints, descending to the earth, and taking possession of it, now restored to Eden beauty and eternal grandeur. This harmonizes with that broad declaration of Christ: "No man hath ascended up into heaven at any time."—John iii, 13. That God would thus populate the world with immortal inhabitants, He fixed by decree before He made it at all; "In hope of eternal life, which God, that cannot lie, promised before the world began." That there are a few passages which speak as though men, Christians, had eternal life now; but there are none which positively assert this; if they did, they would flatly contradict all this array of positive Scripture; but we must take into the account, the fact that whatever is a subject of fiat or decree, and which does not depend upon the will of another, God speaks of as existing before it does actually exist. As an illustration, Christ is said to be a Lamb, slain from the foundation of the world, whereas, He was not actually slain until four thousand years afterward. God said to David, as a prophet, and in reference to Christ, "Thou art My Son, this day I have begotten thee;" when, in fact, He was not exactly thus begotten until a thousand years afterward. Upon the subject, Paul gives us this rule: "God, who quickeneth the dead, calleth those things which be not (yet) as though they were."—Rom. iv, 17.

What Things are Subjects of God's Decrees.

There are certain things which were fixed by the irrevocable decrees of the Almighty before He made the world, and which would be necessary for Him to do, or have done, in order to accomplish His design with the world and its inhabitants. Christ was to be born into temporal life; He was also to be born again from the dead into eternal life, and to render this possible, He was to die. His saints were also to be resurrected to immortality and eternal life. The world was to be re-created or restored, and thus adapted for their everlasting abode; hence, He also promised, "I will come and bring My Father with Me, and we will make our abode with you." This is to be accomplished, as He inspired Isaiah thus to write: "Lo, I come, and My reward is with Me, and My work before Me." We cannot fail to see that the question of immortality being thus settled by the Scriptures themselves, without the intervention of human opinion, also settles another question in relation to future rewards and punishment, and shows that neither are awarded until the last great judgment; and relieves the subject of the absurdity of taking Abel out of heaven, where he has been enjoying unutterable felicity for six thousand years, arraigning him before the judgment-seat of Christ, and compelling him to give an account for the deeds he had done in the body. Also, in releasing Cain from hell's torments, where he had suffered six thousand years, bringing him before the judgment-seat, trying him, to show it to be just that he should be condemned as the murderer of his brother, after which, to send him back forever and ever. By the way, instead of the coming of the judgment being a dreadful event to the wicked, as the Bible represents it, it will be a grand event for poor Cain, giving him a short respite from these torments. Besides, what kind of justice is that which gives Cain, the first murderer, six thousand years longer punishment than the last murderer of the world can possibly have? Hence, the rewards and punishments of Christianity, are given at the judgment, while those of Pagan philosophy, are awarded as every man dies.

This not a New Doctrine.

This cannot be called a new doctrine, for we have shown it to be as old as the Bible; besides, it was held by the two greatest modern reformers, Luther and Wesley. There is not a scrap of evidence in the writings of Luther, to show that he believed anyone went to heaven or hell before the judgment, and he did say this: "I permit the Pope to make dunghill decretals for himself and his faithful, such as, that the soul is immortal, and that he is God upon earth." Upon this subject, we quote the following from John Wesley: "It is, indeed, very generally believed that the souls of good men, as soon as they are discharged from the body, go directly to heaven; but this opinion has not the least foundation in the oracles of God."—"Wesley's Sermon on the Rich Man and Lazarus," vol. 11, page 416. We, however, take no man as authority. The only question with us is, what saith the Scriptures? What has God revealed?

The Immortal Change of the Living Saints at the Last Day.

We cannot do justice to this subject, without presenting the argument, drawn from the change those are to pass through who are alive upon the earth, when the time arrives for its accomplishment. Christ refers to these, in the conversation he had with Martha, at the grave of Lazarus. "Jesus said unto her, thy brother shall rise again. Martha said unto Him, I know that he shall rise again in the resurrection at the last day. Jesus said unto her, I am the resurrection, and the life; he that believeth in Me, though he were dead, yet shall he live; and whosoever liveth, (at that time,) and believeth in Me, shall never die." John xi, 23—26. Paul brings out the subject more fully, thus: "Behold, I show you a mystery; we shall not all sleep (or die,) but we shall all be changed, (whether living or dead,) in a moment—in the twinkling of an eye, at the last trump; for the trumpet shall sound, and the dead shall be raised incorruptable, and we shall be changed; for this corruptable must put on incorruption, aud this mortal must put on immortality."—1 Cor. xv, 51—53.

THE TWO ADAMS. ONE GIVING DEATH; THE OTHER, LIFE.

Here are men, as it is taught, who have mortal life, derived from Adam; this life is temporary. But here is Christ, the second Adam, the Lord from heaven, and He gives His saints another life, which is immortal and eternal. This puts an end to the corruptible, mortal life inherited from Adam. That life, made the first Adam and his offspring, "mortal souls," just as he was himself; for a man cannot transmit what he does not possess. But the life Christ now gives, is immortal and eternal, making those who receive it, immortal souls.

"Neither can they die any more, being the children of the resurrection." Here, as we understand it, is the only true doctrine of "The immortality of the soul;" but, out of Christ, there is no immortality or eternal life, and not in Him, or by Him, until the resurrection of life; and then to be conferred upon the righteous only. If men derive immortal souls from the first Adam, then Christ, the second Adam, confers nothing, for this is all He promises to His saints; therefore, Christ is of no importance to mankind. Indeed, Adam is superior, as he gives immortality to all, whether wicked or righteous, while Christ proposes to confer it upon the righteous only.

THE PLATONIC DISTRIBUTION OF SOULS.

Besides, as the first Adam is not a creator, and therefore cannot make souls, and yet, if he transmits them to his posterity, they must have been all incorporated into his own physical or spiritual constitution, and by natural generation, distributed to each member of the human family as they were born into the world, each in the succession inheriting one soul less; but if this is the fact, then every human being who might have been born and was not, the soul that belonged to it must have died, and this brings it in conflict with its immortality, by supposing it susceptible of death. We admit that this is a very complicated case, but we are only endeavoring to make the best possible case out of it, of which we are capable, and if it is still too complicated to be credible, it is not our fault, but that of the theory. The philosophy of Plato is less complicated, and as he was the author of this whole theory of natural immortality, we had better adopt it, if we cannot take that of Christ and Paul.

He held, as we have seen, that God, the Supreme, made another subordinate deity or geni, and committed to him the work of making souls for men; so He took a cup and mixed soul matter, and after He made souls for all the planets, He had some of it left, from which He made the souls for men, all at once, and imposed the duty on the subordinate deity to distribute one to each male who was born into the world; but He made none for females; they have no souls, according to this heathen philosophy, and therefore, are considered the mere slaves of men.

Death not Death, but Separation—The Doctrine of the Devil.

The philosophy of Plato, however, only suggests the question of the comparative superiority of his geni, and our deity, Adam, in the business and management of the distribution of souls; for it must be remembered that

Adam is not dead, but has become a god, who cannot die, just as the devil told him, if he would only obey him; for as his soul was his life, and that was immortal, of course it could not die, for nothing but life can die. The soul, or life of Adam, only moved out of a clay tenement, into some other more congenial house, perhaps, and the body, or tenement, was never alive; if it had been, it might have lived after the immortal soul had moved out, and if the body never lived, it never could have died, and if it never died, it could never be raised from the dead; there is, therefore, no resurrection of the body; and if the soul never died, then there is no resurrection of the soul, and if the spirit never died, then it cannot be raised from the dead, and therefore, there is no resurrection of the dead at all, and as Christ is not risen from the dead, He is still dead, and Christianity is a specious lie. Hence, we are driven to accept the heathen doctrine of natural immortality, and reject Christianity, or hold to that of Jesus and the resurrection, which we propose to do, and with all the ability with which God has endowed us, endeavor to pull down these strongholds of satan, behind which he has entrenched himself ever since his infernal foot trod the unstained soil of Eden, and gave birth to the father-lie of the world.

> " Ye shall not surely die,
>   Said one of old ;
> And that same cunning lie
>   The priests have told."

Consciousness after Death, Wholly Supported by Inference.—Location of Paradise.

That men are conscious after death, is wholly supported by a few passages which only admit of inference, and we propose not only to show, but when properly understood by taking everything said in connection with them into consideration, that they admit of no such inference, but add confirmation to our view. The first of these we will examine is, what Christ said to the thief on the cross, thus: "And he said unto Jesus, Lord, remember me when thou comest into thy kingdom; and Jesus said unto him, verily, I say unto thee to-day, shalt thou be with Me in paradise."—Luke xxiii, 42—43.

It will be observed that we have changed the comma from after the word "*thee,*" in the answer of Jesus to the prayer, and placed it after the word "day." It must be remembered that the punctuation of the Bible was the work of man, and only done about three hundred years ago. This change, however, is not necessary in order to show that the passage is in harmony with all others referring to paradise, it only conveys the idea taught, more readily.

The penitent did not ask the Lord to remember him on that day in which both were crucified, but it was, "When thou comest into thy kingdom." It is fair to presume from this intelligent prayer, that the thief understood from Jesus, and probably from His discussion of the subject with Pilate, concerning His kingdom, that it was not of this world. "Now is My kingdom, not from hence," it does not now begin, "*Hereafter* shall the Son of Man sit on the right of the power of God," etc. He was the "Nobleman traveling into a far country to receive for himself a kingdom, and to return," "Who shall judge the quick and the dead, at His appearing and His kingdom."—2 Tim. iv, 1. In answer to the prayer, Jesus said, "Verily, I say unto thee to-day, thou shalt be with Me when I come into My kingdom, (and that kingdom is paradise, the New Heavens and the New Earth,) in which, with all My saints, I shall reign forever and ever. Then, verily thou shalt be with Me." We have already shown that Jesus Christ, the Lord, died, and lay in the grave three days from the crucifixion, and therefore, the grave must be paradise, if He went into it on the day of His crucifixion.

For an answer to the inquiry, what it was that ascended into heaven, Paul declares: "It was the same that ascended, that first descended into the lower parts of the earth," (grave.) Three days after this, he said, "Touch Me not, for I have not yet ascended to My Father." In fact, He did not leave the world until forty days afterward, and then we have the history of His ascension. Thus, everything in the Great Book is consistent, harmonious and intelligible, if we do not become wiser than its Author and assume to teach infinite wisdom. This is the very strongest passage upon which the Paganized, Papal, holy fathers tortured, to make it teach an intermediate place or state, called purgatory.

Another of the passages containing the name paradise, is the following: "To him that overcometh will I give to eat of the tree of life, which is in the midst of the paradise of God." That the tree of life here, is a type of Christ, cannot be correct, for the reason that those who are to eat of it are those who overcome, and are the immortal inhabitants of the New Heavens and New Earth, and that they thus overcame, was, by eating Christ's flesh and drinking His blood; or literally, who had been saved by belief in His death and resurrection, of which this was the result. That they had overcome by Christ's grace, gave them a right to partake or eat of the "Tree of life." The Christian warfare is limited to the present life; for there can be no strife among the dead, no belief or unbelief, in the grave. There, where once their Savior and Lord lay, shall the flesh of the saints also rest, in hope of a "better resurrection." When God gave Job this inspired picture of his hope, he exclaimed, in ecstasy and enrapt interest, lest it should not be written and transmitted to the ages, "O that my words were now written! O, that they were printed in a book! that they were graven with an iron pen, and lead (leaded) in the rock forever! For I know that my Redeemer liveth, and that He shall stand at the latter day upon the earth; and though after my skin worms destroy this body, yet in my flesh shall I see God, whom I shall see for myself, and mine eyes shall behold (Him) and not another."—Job xix, 23—27.

That this is the time when those who "overcome" expected to be put in possession of their reward, and not at death, is also clearly shown by the closing words of the Spirit to this church, namely, that then they were to be given to eat of the tree of life, which was in the midst of the paradise of God. The question to be considered, in order to understand this passage, and truth, is, where is paradise; for the tree of life grew in its midst, and if we can understand the location of the one, it will also be that of the other.

In the first place, we remark, that the first two chapters of the Bible contain the history of the Eden World. "And God planted a garden eastward in Eden, (in the east of the Eden world,) and there He put the man whom He had formed, and out of the ground made the Lord God to grow, the tree of life, and every tree that is pleasant to the sight, and good for food."—Gen ii, 8, 9. After the fatal fall, we read: "And the Lord God said, behold, the man is become as one of us, to know good and evil; and now, lest he put forth his hand, and take also of the tree of life, and eat, and live forever; therefore, the Lord God sent him forth from the garden of Eden, and placed at the east of the garden of Eden, cherubims and a flaming sword, which turned every way, to keep the way of the tree of life."—Gen. iii, 24.

That the world is to be restored to its Eden beauty and perfection, and that this determination God has caused every prophet to write, He ever inspired, we need only quote one passage to prove: "Repent ye, therefore, and be converted, that your sins may be blotted out, when the times of refreshing shall come from the presence of the Lord; for He shall send Jesus Christ, which before was preached unto you, whom the heaven must receive, until the times of *restitution of all things*, which God hath spoken by the mouth of all His holy prophets since the world began."—Acts iii, 19—21.

Perhaps we should quote one passage more, in this connection, which shows the manner of Christ's reception into heaven, as here stated, and of His coming, again, to thus restore the world, according to the universal voice of prophesy, which is this: "And when He had spoken these things, while they beheld, he was taken up; and a cloud received Him out of their sight. And while they looked steadfastly toward heaven as He went up, behold, two men stood by them in white apparel, which also said, ye men of Galilee, why stand ye gazing up into heaven?

This same Jesus, which is taken up from you into heaven, shall so come in like manner as ye have seen Him go into heaven."—Acts i, 9—11. We may also remark, that the last two chapters of the Bible contain the pre-historic record of the world thus restored, re-created, and with the curse taken away. That is the New Heaven and New Earth, constituting "The world to come." The present is the temporary world, to be folded up and changed— changed into the permanent, the eternal. That is the glorious kingdom of God, and when thus restored, it will be given unto the predestined inhabitants, thus: "Then shall the King say unto them on His right hand, come, ye blessed of My Father, inherit the kingdom prepared for you from the foundation of the world."—Matt. xxv, 34. Here, then, is the eternal abode of God, angels and immortal men, of which there is nothing more clearly and fully taught in the Bible. Hence, it is paradise restored.

"And He showed me a pure river of water of life, clear as crystal, proceeding out of the throne of God and the Lamb. In the midst of the street of it, and on either side of the bank of the river, was there the tree of life, which bare twelve manner of fruits, and yielded her fruit every month; and the leaves of the tree were for the healing of the nations. Blessed are they that do His commandments, that they may have right to the tree of life, and enter in through the gates into the city."—Rev. xxii.

Here we have the statements that the tree of life grew in the midst of the paradise of God, and that the tree of life grew in the New Heaven and New Earth; therefore, the New Heaven and New Earth, and paradise, are one and the same place. In relation to the nature of the tree of life, we indulge no speculation, further than that which is written in the Scriptures of truth; to understand this, is the heighth of our ambition, concerning which, one thing is certain, that if Adam had eaten of this tree, he would have lived forever, and would have been an immortal soul, notwithstanding his sin, from which we may learn that it is a very easy thing for God to preserve even human life indefinitely, or make it everlasting life. In other words, that it would be just as easy for God to make a tree or trees grow in the present world, whose chemical properties would possess healing virtue for all physical derangements, and to perpetuate youth, as to have made those whose properties possess the bane or poison of every life, and renders every muscle and fibre of the system slowly or suddenly rigid, immovable and dead.

The only other passage which speaks of paradise, is a vision or revelation, given of it to the Apostle Paul, and which, as we shall see, confirms this view of its location. He says: "It is not expedient for me doubtless to glory. I will come to visions and revelations of the Lord. I knew a man in Christ above fourteen years ago, (whether in the body, I cannot tell, or whether out of the body, I cannot tell; God knoweth;) such a one caught up to the *third heaven*, and I knew such a man, (whether in the body, or out of the body, I cannot tell; God knoweth;) how that he was caught up into paradise, and heard unspeakable words, which it is impossible for a man to utter."—2 Cor. xii, 1—4. Here we see that the place, as the scene of this vision and revelation, is called paradise, and also the third heaven. Now, if we can find the location of the third heaven, it will be also that of paradise. We have already seen that paradise was the New Heaven and New Earth—the world to come, and succeeds that which now exists. The question is, does the Bible contain evidence for calling the "New Heaven" the third heaven. Let us turn to the Epistle of Peter, and we will find the following: "For this they willingly are ignorant of, that by the Word of God the heavens were of old, and the earth standing out of the water and in the water; whereby, the world that then was, being overflowed with water, perished." Here was the first heaven, the Eden World, and this perished; the flood so deranged that once beautiful globe, breaking up its entire surface, under the second curse of God, so that the present world compares so poorly with that, that it justifies the apostolic declaration, "The heaven and the earth which then were, 'perished;' but the heavens and the earth which are now, by the same word, (doomed by the Word of God,) are kept in store, reserved unto fire against the day of judgment and perdition of ungodly men." Here is the second heaven and earth destined to pass the ordeal of a universal conflagration. "Looking for, and hasting unto the coming of the day of God, wherein the heavens, being on fire, shall be dissolved, and the elements shall melt with fervent heat. Nevertheless, we, according to His promise, look for New Heavens and a New Earth, wherein dwelleth righteousness."—Chapter iii. Here, then, we have God's definition and locality of the third heaven, and of paradise.

After the burning of the present world and its re-creation into the world to come, as God promised, in the restoration of all things, the Revelator gives us the following: "Death and hell were cast into the lake of fire, this is the second death, and whosoever was not found written in the Book of Life was cast into the lake of fire. And I saw a New Heaven and a New Earth, for the first heaven and the first earth were past away." This first heaven passed away with the burning day, just as the Eden heaven and earth passed away with the flood. "And I heard a great voice out of heaven, saying, behold, the tabernacle of God is with men, and He will dwell with them, and they shall be His people, and God himself shall be with them and be their God; and He that sat upon the throne said, behold, I make all things new. And He said unto me, write, for these Words are true and faithful." Here is the third heaven—the New Heavens and the New Earth of Peter's prediction and Paul's vision, "In which dwelleth righteousness, or in which the righteous forever dwell, not with the Spirit of God, but with 'God himself.'"

In regard to the words Paul heard in his vision, and which it was impossible to utter, in John's revelation he heard the same; and it was more fully brought out by the latter. "And I looked, and lo, a Lamb stood on Mount Zion, and with Him a hundred and forty and four thousand, having their Father's name written in their foreheads. And I heard a voice from heaven, as the voice of many waters, and as the voice of a great thunder; and I heard the voice of harpers, harping with their harps; and they sung as it were a new song before the throne, and no man could learn that song, but the hundred and forty and four thousand which were redeemed from the earth." —Rev. xiv.

No man could utter the words heard by Paul, and no man could learn the words John heard sung. The place where Paul, in vision, heard them, was paradise and the third heaven. The place where John also heard them, in vision, was paradise, the third and New Heaven. With the curse taken away from the present world, and it restored to its original and paradisiacal beauty, and eternal duration. God's everlasting kingdom, established under the whole heaven, in which, when Christ comes into it, He is pledged to remember the thief, and admit him, with himself, into His kingdom.

The Transfiguration, a Vision of Final Glory Beyond the Resurrection.

Another of the passages which is supposed to teach that the dead are alive, is that of the transfiguration. This was a vision of Christ's, and the saints' appearance, when in their final glory, or when He comes into His kingdom, and in answer to the prayer, "Glorify thou Me with the glory I had with thee before the world was, *with thine own self;* then came a voice from heaven, saying, I have both glorified thee, and will also glorify thee again." The glory of His presence was so overwhelming, that when he spoke, the Revelator says: "I fell at His feet as dead." It is when He thus comes in His glory and kingdom, of which He gave some of His disciples a vision, in which He was transfigured. This is recorded as follows: "There be some standing here, which shall not taste of death till they see the Son of Man coming in His kingdom; and after six days, Jesus taketh Peter, James, and John, his brother, and bringeth them up into a high mountain apart, and was transfigured before them; and His face did shine as the sun, and His raiment was white as the light. And behold, there appeared Moses and Elias, talking with Him. Then answered Peter, and said unto Jesus, Lord, it is good for us to be here; if thou wilt, let us make here three tabernacles; one for thee, and one for Moses, and one for Elias. While he yet spake, behold, a bright cloud overshadowed them; and behold, a voice out of the cloud, which said, this is My beloved Son, in whom I am well pleased; hear ye Him. And when the disciples heard it, they fell on their faces and were sore afraid; and Jesus came and touched them, and said, arise, and be not afraid; and when they had lifted up their eyes, they saw no man, save Jesus only. And as they came down from the mountain, Jesus charged them, saying, tell the *vision* to no man, until the Son of Man be risen from the dead."—Chapter xvi, 27, 28, and chapter xvii, 1—9.

"Trans" is a Latin preposition, used in English as a prefix, and signifies, over, beyond; the word transfiguration, therefore, means to pass over into a form beyond— to appear in a form which, at the time, does not exist, but which will exist in the future.

Here the three disciples, the " *some*," of them who should not taste of death until they saw the Son of Man coming into His kingdom, according to Christ's promise, saw, in vision, Christ transfigured into that glorified form He will wear when He comes in the clouds of heaven with power and great glory, as He told the disciples, six days before, in which they should see Him. Now, as He did not then come, in reality, into His kingdom of power and glory, and is to thus come at the end of the world, therefore, the vision on the Mount, was these future scenes. They saw Moses and Elias living, having, as they will have at that time, come forth unto the resurrection of life. As they lay upon their faces, overpowered with the glory, Jesus came and touched them, and the vision was gone, and there was no man there but Jesus, and themselves. Luke says: " And behold, there talked with Him, two men, which were Moses and Elias, who appeared *in glory*, and spoke of His decease which He should accomplish at

Jerusalem." Here Moses and Elias, as well as Christ, appeared in their glory. They were also transfigured into their resurrection, glorious form, and which will not take place until Christ comes in His glory, as is thus written: "For our conversation is in heaven, from whence also we look for the Saviour, the Lord Jesus Christ, who shall change our vile body, that it may be fashioned like unto His *glorious body*, according to the working whereby He is able even to subdue all things unto himself."—Phil. iii. 20—21. "It is sown in dishonor; it is raised in glory." —1 Cor. xv, 43.

Now, that Moses is not an exception to those who are to be glorified at the resurrection, (indeed, this comprehends all the saints,) we introduce a passage, whereby Christ and Moses both show that it takes place at this event: "And Jesus answered and said unto them, the children of this world marry, and are given in marriage; but they which shall be accounted worthy to obtain that World, and the resurrection from the dead, neither marry, nor are given in marriage; neither can they die any more; for they are the children of God, being the children of the resurrection. And that the dead are raised, even Moses showed, at the bush, when he called the Lord, the God of Abraham, and the God of Isaac, and the God of Jacob, for He is not the God of the dead, but of the living."— Luke xx, 34—38.

When are the Saints the Children of God?

Here we have the argument that the children of God are the children of the resurrection, because, from thenceforth they live, and cease to be dead, for He is not the God of the dead, but He is the God of the living. Abraham, Isaac, Jacob and Moses are dead, and will remain dead until the resurrection, therefore, He is not their God now, and will not be while they are dead, for He is not the God of the dead; but as God is here declared to be their God, and as He is only the God of the living, resurrected saints, therefore, these dead men must live again. Hence, Moses showed the resurrection, by calling Him the God of Abraham, Isaac and Jacob, and whom he knew were dead, hence, must live again. Until this resurrection of glory, honor, immortality and eternal life, the saints are the children of God, by faith; that is, they believe they shall then be God's children. Until then, they receive the "*spirit of adoption*, whereby we cry, Abba, Father; the Spirit itself beareth witness with our Spirit, that we are the children of God; and if children, then heirs—heirs of God, and joint heirs with Christ, if so be that we suffer with Him; that we may be also glorified together; for I reckon that the sufferings of this present time are not worthy to be compared with the glory which shall be revealed in us."—Rom. viii, 15—18. The glory is to be revealed in us, in our resurrection into Christ's glorious image. It is true, the saints are here called the children of God; but the whole passage shows that the relation is one only of heirship, which waits for the inheritance, and it is to be awarded when Christ comes to be glorified in His saints. "We shall be glorified together," Moses included. Verse 23, we read thus: " Because the creature itself shall also be delivered from the bondage of corruption, into the glorious liberty of the children of God, (the resurrection from corruption to incorruption,) for we know that the whole creation groaneth and travaileth in pain together, until now; and not only they, but ourselves also, which have the first fruits of the Spirit ; even we ourselves groan within ourselves, waiting for the adoption, to wit, the redemption of our body." Here Paul declares that himself and all the saints have the spirit of adoption only, and all have a voice in the universal groaning for the adoption itself, which he explains to be the redemption of our body. Then shall God be the God of Abraham and of Isaac, of Jacob and of Moses, and all the saints, because from that time forth "all live unto God."

That it was the vision of the coming of Christ in His glory that was seen on the Mount of Transfiguration, is further proved by what Peter testifies concerning it, in his 2d Epistle: "For we have not followed cunningly-devised fables, when we made known unto you the power and coming of our Lord Jesus Christ, but were eye witnesses of His majesty; for He received from God, the Father, honor and glory, when there came such voice to Him from the excellent glory; this is My beloved Son, in whom I am well pleased; and this voice, which came from heaven, we heard, when we were with Him in the Holy Mount." —1st, 16—18.

How to Determine the Chronology of Events.

In reference to the statement in the record of this vision, that Moses and Elias talked with Christ concerning His approaching sufferings at Jerusalem, we may remark, that it is a very common thing in Scripture visions and revelations, to talk of things past, present, and future, as though they existed at the time they were seen. Hence, the angel of Jesus said to John, "I will show thee things which were, and are, and are to come." The chronological order of events, in any given vision, must be determined by the nature and description of the events themselves, contained in any part of the Bible where the same subject is brought to view, every witness must be consulted, in order to arrive at the exact truth. In this vision, therefore, Christ and these two saints appeared glorified, and in His glorious kingdom, when it comes in power.

Elijah Died, in Common with all Men.

It is supposed that in the case of the prophet Elijah, or Elias, that he is with God in heaven: but Christ said, "No man hath ascended up into heaven, but the Son of Man, who came down from heaven." Hence, Elijah did not go there. The history of his ascension is as follows: "And it came to pass, as they still went on, and talked, that behold, there appeared a chariot of fire, and horses of fire, and parted them both asunder, (Elijah and Elisha,) and Elijah went up by a whirlwind, into heaven. And Elisha saw it, and he cried, my father, my father; the chariot of Israel and the horsemen thereof; and he saw him no more."—2 Kings ii, 11, 12. Here Elijah went up into the atmosphere, firmament, called heaven; but not into the heaven where Christ is. That Elijah died, is also certain from this Scripture testimony: "Sin entered into the world, and death by sin, and so death passed upon *all men*, for all have sinned."

"As in Adam *all die*, even so in Christ shall all be made alive; but every one in his own order; Christ the first fruits, afterward they that are Christ's at His coming." Elijah, therefore, died, and he did not receive his resurrection, as Christ was the first fruits of them that slept, and Elijah is yet dead with the rest of the saints, waiting his resurrection. Paul, speaking of all the prophets, of which Elijah was one, says: "*These all died* in faith, not having received the promises, but having seen them afar off, and were persuaded of them, and embraced them, and confessed that they were strangers and pilgrims on the earth, that they might obtain a better resurrection."—Heb. xi. That he was a common, fallen mortal, is asserted thus: "Elias was a man subject to like passions as we are."—James v, 17.

Enoch Died also, and Awaits his Resurrection and Translation.

It is also supposed that Enoch, who was translated, did not die; but if we carefully examine what is said of him, and what the expressions mean, we shall find that there are no grounds for the belief. "And Enoch walked with God, and he was not, for God took him."—Gen. v, 24. In the first place, the expression, "he was not," means that he died. "And they said, thy servants are twelve brethren, the sons of one man in the land of Canaan; and behold, the youngest is this day with our father, and one, *is not.*"—Gen. xlii, 13. The one that "is not," was Joseph, whom they supposed was dead. "Our fathers have sinned, and *are not;* and we have borne their iniquities."—Lam. v, 7. "Are not," declares they were dead, which was the fact. So Enoch "was not." "God took him," not to heaven, but out of the world of life.

"I pray not that thou shouldst take them out of the world, but that thou shouldst keep them from the evil."—John xvii, 15. Christ prays that God would not take His children out of the world, out of life, as He took Enoch. The following passages show that Enoch died the same as other men: "Wherefore, as by one man, sin entered into the world, and death by sin; and so death passed upon *all men*, for that all have sinned. Nevertheless, death reigned from Adam to Moses, (Enoch was in this period;) even over them who had not sinned after the similitude of Adam's transgression."—Rom. v, 12, 14. Here is Paul's testimony, and settles the question that all of Adam's posterity sin and die, and that death passed upon Enoch as one of the "all men." Now, let us see what else Paul has to say concerning this case. "By faith, Enoch was translated, that he should not see death; and was not found, because God had translated him; for, before his translation, he had this testimony, that he pleased God."—Heb. ii, 5. The word "translation," means to change one thing into another, and in this case, we think, from mortality to immortality, and into the kingdom of God; and to show that Enoch was to be thus translated, and that he was not an exception, but that all the saints share equally in the same translation; and at the same time, we quote again from Paul: "Giving thanks unto the Father, which hath made us meet to be partakers of the inheritance of the saints in light; who hath delivered us from the power of darkness, and hath *translated us* into the kingdom of His dear Son."—Col. i, 12, 13. The inheritance of the saints in light, is the New Heavens and New Earth; this is also the destined kingdom of God's dear Son; and the way into that, is the immortal resurrection; and by faith in Jesus Christ the saints have obtained a fitness for that inheritance. The truth, therefore, here taught, is, that having this faith, and which pleases God, "For without faith it is impossible to please God," all His saints have the promise that they shall be translated into the kingdom of God, when that kingdom comes, and while they live in the world, they are translated into it by faith; that is, they believe they will be thus translated. Hence,

"By faith, Enoch was translated, and it was that he should not see death, (the second death.)" His name, with that of Abel and all the ancient saints, was written "in the Lamb's Book of Life, slain from the foundation of the world." "And another Book was opened, which is the Book of Life, and whosoever was not found written in the Book of Life was cast into the lake of fire." This is the second death. Hence, by faith, Enoch was translated, that he should not see the second death; and if he did not thus die, he cannot be raised from the dead. The opposite supposition is absurd.

After referring to Abel, Enoch, Noah, Moses and other notable saints, Paul declares, "These all *died in faith*, not having received the promises, (things promised,) but having seen them afar off, and were persuaded of them, and embraced them, and confessed that they were strangers and pilgrims on the earth."—Heb. xi, 13. He also adds, "That they might obtain a better resurrection."—Verse 35. Here it is declared Enoch died in the faith that looked for a better resurrection, a better one than the wicked will have, through which he would be translated into the kingdom of God's dear Son, with all the other saints. The expression of Paul, "He hath (present tense) translated us into the kingdom of God's dear Son," is explained by the fact that it was by faith; they have the faith that it would be accomplished, when and according to the promise of God.

No Man Ever Went to God in Heaven.

The words of Christ, "No man hath ascended up into heaven," are not at variance with what is declared of Elijah and Enoch, and these cases, therefore, afford no evidence for the conscious existence of the dead.

The Laws of Physiology and the Bible, Harmonize.

In conclusion, we propose to show from the physiological laws of organic man, that when he dies, and whether it is defined to be death, or the separation of the mind and body, that all intellectual power as absolutely perishes as though it had never existed; and, without a resurrection, which is really a new creation, will so forever remain. As introductory even to this purely scientific argument, we quote three passages of Scripture: "Whatsoever thy hand findeth to do, do it with thy might, for there is no work, nor device, nor knowledge, nor wisdom, in the grave, whither *thou goest*, (not his spirit, but the man himself.)"—Eccl. ix, 10. "For the living know that they shall die, but the dead know not anything."—Verse 5. "Put not your trust in princes, nor in the son of man, in whom there is no help; his breath goeth forth, he returneth to his earth; in that very day his thoughts perish."—Ps. cxlvi, 4.

Physiology Connected with this Question.

Man is generally represented as composed of body; soul or life; spirit and mind, which includes his moral powers, also called "the heart." The bodily division may be denominated the anatomical house, which contains, and to which are internally attached, the organs of life called vital, and those of intellect. If we except the spinal column, we may say that any part of this bodily case may be, and has been, carried off without destroying the life or intellectual faculties of the individual. We do not mean that the whole of these parts may be destroyed from a single individual, but that different parts from different individuals. For example, all the limbs have been amputated, portions of the ribs and sides; indeed, all but those portions to which the vital organs are attached; all parts of the cranium, the ears, nose, lips, jaws, cheeks, eyes, tongue, and skin, as well as one lobe of the brain, and without destroying life or intellect, thus demonstrating that none of these parts constitute the living or knowing faculties. It is, however, just as certain that this house is essential to the existence of life and intelligence, as that these exist at all. We may mention two facts in proof of this:

First.—The vital organs are so hung to, and connected with the internal case, that to loose the attachment, would produce instant death.

Second.—The spinal column constitutes part of the case itself; and further than this, it may be added, that the nerves branching from it, connect with all the organs of life and involuntary motion, and convey the electrical force from the brain to all, by which they are enabled to perform their various functions.

The body, therefore, thus defined, although no part of the phenomena of life and intelligence, yet without it, neither can exist.

What is the Soul?

The second department of man, we are to consider, is life, and in an unlimited sense, comprehending the whole man, called "a living soul;" the question, therefore, is, what are we to understand by life? As our example of investigation, let us take the first man that lived, the short account of whose creation, is thus given: "And the Lord God formed man of the dust of the ground, and breathed into his nostrils the breath of life; and the man became a living soul."—Gen. ii, 7. Mark, it was not life which was breathed into him, but the *breath of life;* neither was it a living soul, forced into him; but the formation and the animating breath made the man himself "the living soul." Nothing is more certain, both from physiological necessity and this language, than that it was common atmospheric air which was breathed into Adam; this, and nothing else, is man's "breath of life," as well as the breath of the life of every other animal; give them access to this, and if their vital organs are perfectly developed, they will live; but prevent the air from entering the lungs through the mouth or nostrils, and no matter how perfectly they are developed, they will never see life. Suppose it was a living, thinking being, or substance, which was breathed into man, and which dwelt in his organization as a tenant in a house, it would not have been life to him, as it would not have been his lungs, or heart, or the atmosphere, which are constituents of his life; besides this, Adam would have lived after his formation, by breathing common air, and he would also have been a thinking, feeling creature. Now, if another thinking, feeling creature had been forced into his organization, there would have been two thinking, feeling creatures merged in one, and each would have preserved his own personal identity, and each have a will; for any thinking, intelligent thing, or substance, must have a will, and this again argues individual responsibility; hence, we have two independent beings, or call them what you please, dwelling in one body, but not incorporated into each other, as the life of one is not that of the other.

WHAT IS THE MEANING OF SPIRIT?

It is scarcely necessary to consider the spirit of man as a separate object, for it must be obvious from what has already been said, that the spirit is simply atmospheric air, when entering an organic formation, made in accordance with the laws of life, so that it will animate all, and bring the thing to life, and it is precisely the same, whether in the lower animals or man, so far as life is concerned; and it is as proper to say, a spirited horse, as a spirited man; and it is as proper to call the animating properties of wine, "the spirit of wine," as it is to designate the animating principle of man or beast, the principle of either. It is also as proper to designate the affections of the lower animal, spiritual, as those of the higher animal, man; and the terms lower and higher, express the only difference, that of degree. The lower organic creature—and it is in the scale of organism that makes it lower—having no thoughts high enough to take in the conception of its Maker, or even that it had a Maker, and, consequently, of any moral relations existing between them.

The spirit, coming from the atmospheric heavens, ascends by its specific gravity, while the solids of the animal, for the same reason, return to the ground; both to the localities from whence they were taken. "The Lord God formed man of the dust of the ground, and breathed into his nostrils the *breath of life*, and the man became a living soul."—Gen. ii, 7. "Behold, I do bring a flood of waters upon the earth, to destroy all flesh, wherein is the breath of life."—Chapter vi, 17. "And all flesh died that moved upon the earth, both of fowl and cattle, and of every creeping thing, in whose nostrils was the breath of life, both man and cattle, and creeping thing died."—Chapter vii, 21. Here man and every living thing had, in common, in its nostrils, the breath of life, and though it is not said of the lower animals, as in the case of Adam, that God breathed it into them, yet it is just as certain that He did it, as it is that they had it; and in each case it was the breath of life, and was in their nostrils, which means simply that they inhaled and exhaled the air, or breathed the breath of life.

"And it came to pass, that the son of the woman, the mistress of the house, fell sick; and his sickness was so sore, that there was no breath left in him."—1 Kings xvii, 17. "In whose hand is the soul of every living thing, (every living thing has a soul, then,) and the breath of all mankind."—Job xii, 10. "The Spirit of God hath made me, and the breath of the Almighty hath given me life."—Job xxxiii, 4. The wind and air are often called the breath of the Lord. Here is an instance: "The channels of the sea appeared; the foundations of the world were discovered, at the rebuking of the Lord, at the blast of the breath of His nostrils."—2 Sam. xxii, 16. Here is another: "Thou didst blow with thy wind; the sea covered them; with the blast of thy nostrils the waters were gathered together, the floods stood upright as a heap, and the depths were congealed in the heart of the sea."—Ex. xv, 8, 12. Here we have the fact stated, that it was the wind, the air, the breath of God, represented as breathing through His nostrils, by which He divided the waters of the Red Sea, which He also breathed into Adam, and into every beast, and moving, creeping thing, upon the earth; all have it in common, and which is the "breath of life" of everything that lives.

"By the breath of God, frost is given, and the breath of the waters is straightened."—Job. xxxvii, 10. Here the breath of God is *cold air*. "His breath kindleth coals, and a flame goeth out of His mouth."—Job xli, 21. Here God's breath is hot air, and not immortality.

"By the Word of the Lord were the heavens made, and all the host of them by the breath of His mouth."—Ps. xxxiii, 6. It is here the same thing as the Spirit of God. "And the Spirit of God moved upon the face of the waters."—Gen. i, 2. "Thou hidest thy face, they are troubled; thou takest away their breath, they die, and return to their dust. Thou sendeth forth thy Spirit, they are created; and thou renewest the face of the earth."—Ps. civ, 29, 30. It is the breath of life; take it away, and therefore, "they die." His breath goeth forth, he returneth to his earth; in that very day his thoughts perish."—Ps. cxlvi, 4. He can no more breathe, and he dies, and when he dies, his power to think, perishes; and as Paul declares, will remain perished until the resurrection, even all those which have fallen asleep in Christ.

"I said in mine heart, God shall judge the righteous and the wicked; for there is a time there for every purpose and for every work. I said in mine heart, concerning the estate of the sons of men, that God might manifest them, and that they might see that they themselves are beasts. For that which befalleth the sons of men, befalleth beasts; even one thing befalleth them; as the one dieth, so dieth the other; yea, they all have one breath; so that a man hath no pre-eminence above a beast; all go unto one place; all are of the dust, and all turn to dust again. Who knoweth the spirit of a man, that goeth upward, and the spirit of a beast, that goeth downward to the earth?"—Eccl. iii, 18—21. Here we have the facts stated, that so far as the life, death, and breath, or spirit of a man and the lower animals are concerned, he has no pre-eminence above them; both have the same natural life, both have the same spirit, both die alike, both go to the same place, both turn to dust; perfectly refuting the notion that the spirit of man goeth upward, and the spirit of a beast goeth downward to the earth, and which the very expression admits to be the same which the heathen pretended to know was a fact; nay, they both go to the dust and await the resurrection and the judgment at the last day, just as this passage sets forth. The only going up of the spirit, and it applies equally to man or beast, is, the gravity of the atmospheric breath, and the solids of which they are composed, and which is refuted by the very question itself.

Objection, "Lord Jesus, Receive my Spirit," Considered.

There is a seeming objection to this Scripture, in the words supposed to have been spoken by the martyr Stephen, "Lord Jesus, receive my spirit;" but on close examination, it will be seen that they were uttered in derision of what he had before said about seeing the glory of God, and Jesus standing on the right hand of God. After he had said this, then follows what the persecutors said, thus: "Then they cried out with a loud voice, and stopped their ears, and ran upon him with one accord, and cast him out of the city, and stoned Stephen, calling upon God, and saying, Lord Jesus, receive my spirit." Then follows what Stephen said: "And he kneeled down and cried with a loud voice, Lord, lay not this sin to their charge; and when he had said this, he fell asleep."—Acts vii, 55—60. "Seeing He giveth to all life and breath."—Acts xvii, 25.

Wind, Breath, and Spirit, Meaning the Same.

In order to show still further that the words, wind, breath and spirit, are used interchangeably, not only when describing the present, mortal life, but also the resurrection life of His saints, we introduce Ezekiel's vision of that work, thus: "The hand of the Lord was upon me, and carried me out in the Spirit of the Lord, and set me down in the midst of the valley which was full of bones; and behold, there were very many in the open valley; and lo, they were very dry. And He said unto me, son of man, can these bones live? And I answered, O Lord God, thou knowest. Again He said unto me, prophesy upon these bones, and say unto them, O, ye dry bones, hear ye the Word of the Lord. This saith the Lord God unto these bones, behold, I will cause breath to enter into you, and ye shall live; (this is the same form of expression as 'The Lord God breathed into him the breath of life,' as in the case of Adam,) and I will lay sinews upon you, and I will bring up flesh upon you, and cover you with skin, and put breath in you, and ye shall live; and ye shall know that I am the Lord. So I prophesied as I was commanded; and as I prophesied, there was a noise, and behold, a shaking, and the bones came together, bone to his bone, and when I beheld, lo, the sinews and the flesh came up upon them; but there was no breath in them. (They were in the same organic formation as Adam, before the breath of life was forced into his nostrils; possessing lungs, heart, stomach, liver, and, indeed, every vital organ, without which he could not have drawn the second breath, and, therefore, it could not have been the breath of life to him, or any living thing.) Then said He unto me, prophesy unto the wind, and say to the wind, thus saith the Lord God, come from the four winds, O breath, and breathe upon these slain, that they may live. So I prophesied as He commanded me, and the breath came into them, and they lived, and stood upon their feet, an exceeding great army. Then said He unto me, son of man, these bones are the whole house of Israel. (All who have the faith of Israel, for which reason he was thus named, 'Thy name shall no more be called Jacob, but Israel; for as a prince hast thou power, and hast prevailed with God and man.') Behold, they say, our bones are dried, and our hope is lost; we are cut off for our parts. ('For the hope of the fathers, that there should be a resurrection of the dead, I am called in question of the Jews.'—Paul. 'If there be no resurrection of the dead, then they that have fallen asleep in Christ have perished.'—Paul.) Therefore, prophesy and say unto them, thus saith the Lord God, behold, O my people, I will open your graves, and cause you to come up out of your graves, and bring you into the land of Israel; and ye shall know that I am the Lord, when I have opened your graves, O my people, and brought you up out of your graves, and shall put my Spirit (or breath) in you, and ye shall live, and I shall place you in your own land; then shall ye know that I, the Lord, have spoken it, and performed it, saith the Lord."—Ez. xxxvii, 1—13. This land is the heavenly country promised to Abraham, Isaac and Jacob, and to Abraham's seed, which means Christ, and all who believe in Him, are counted to Abraham for the seed. "They that are of faith are the children of Abraham," therefore, he is the father of the faithful. These all died in the faith, not having received so much of the land promised them for an everlasting possession, as to set a foot on, and they looked for a better resurrection, through which to enter into the heavenly country, the New Heavens and the New Earth. Here we see that which gives the resurrection saints life, is called wind, breath and spirit.

Etymology of the Word Spirit.

The Latin *spiritus*, to breathe, to blow. The primitive sense is, to rush or drive. Primarily, wind, air in motion; hence, breath. "All bodies have spirits and pneumatical parts within them."—Bacon. See Webster.

The most primitive use of the word is in the creation of Adam, and the reason why it has been made to mean anything else, as the animating principle of all living things, is its corruption, to suit the silly notion of heathen philosophy, that man's life is not like the life of other animals, but that it is an immortal, immaterial substance, to which the name spirit has been applied. The pure, original and Bible sense, is, that it describes a material substance, "*wind, breath*," but the modern use of it is, to describe, immateriality, that is "*not* matter," and, therefore, nothing. Now, as nothing but matter can fill any part of space, immateriality has no existence in any part of space; it is, therefore, the strongest possible term to express annihilation; but the first of these definitions is that of the Bible, while the other, and exactly the contrary one, belongs to heathen fables.

THOUGHT DEPENDS UPON LIFE, LIFE UPON ORGANIZATION.

Here, then, we have the physiological divisions of organic man, having a body, enclosing the vital organs and those constituting the mind; these, animated by breathing common atmospheric air, is the spirit of life, resulting from these thus living is, the feeling and thinking being, man. It is obvious, that, if the knowing department is not the living, and it could be separated from it, that it would be incapable of thought, and the man would cease to be intelligent, and so remain, while the living department was dead. Suppose that, after Adam had been formed with all the organs of life, he had been deprived of access to atmospheric air, or that it had not been forced into his lungs, would he have ever had a thought? Or, suppose that breath had been forced into his body, and that it contained no lungs, could he have ever drawn the second breath, and would he not, therefore, have been forever incapable of thought? Is it not also a fact that if the lungs are taken out of a man, that all thought ceases, which would not be the case if the thinking department had life in itself; and if this experiment had been performed upon Adam, would he not have been as incapable of thought, as though the lungs had been left out of his creation?

Here we see that the interdependence of these parts are such, that neither can be dispensed with, and man be capable of thought, and therefore of intelligence. For instance, the voluntary bodily instruments, and anatomical house, are an essential enclosure for the vital organs, holding and suspending them in their relative and necessary positions.

All the Vital Organs Parts of Life.

The vital organs are essential, to enable the man to breathe. The breathing is essential, to oxydize and electrify the blood; indeed, to make it blood at all. The circulation of the blood is essential to life, and the heart is essential to the circulation, and the circulation, to life. The electrical voluntary and involuntary forces are essential, to enable the two sets of nerves to perform their functions, as well as the nerves of sensation, which makes feeling possible. The existence of the two brains, cerebrum and cerebellum, the sources of the voluntary and involuntary nerves, and reservoir of the electrical forces, are also essential to life and thought. The spinal column, with its branching pairs of nerves leading to the vital organs, is the essential medium of communication between the anterior involuntary brain and the organs of life, and the posterior brain and the instruments of locomotion, or volition, as well as to supply this brain with the power to think, and thought is essential to the existence of feeling, feeling to motive, and motive to action.

Here we have an exemplification of the reason why the prophet made the acknowledgment: "For I am fearfully and wonderfully made."—Ps. cxl, 14. And we have the conclusion, that the being receives an impression from the outward world, through one of the five senses, before he thinks; he thinks before he concludes; he concludes before he wills; he wills before he acts; but the brain receives its electric force from the breath, through the lungs, as it has nerves leading to the lungs, as well as the involuntary brain, so that the lungs may continue to breathe when the mind is asleep; the lungs are, therefore, essential, to furnish the brain with the power to think; and all the vital organs are essential, to enable the lungs to inflate and exhale the air; therefore, there can be no thought without life, and no life without organs, and the knowing department of man not being the living department, thought cannot exist when the living department is dead. Hence, the great scientist declared of man: "His breath goeth forth, he returneth to his earth; in that very day his thoughts perish."—Ps. cxlvi, 4. Here we have the science of man's life, death, and intelligence, and as we see, most perfectly, corresponds with the Bible statements of his nature, and these are the only sources of reliable information upon the subject, and perfectly contradict the heathen views, which cannot, therefore, be true.

The advocates for the endless, conscious torments of the wicked, as we have seen, select a few expressions, found in passages, which, at best, only admit of inference in its favor, and either from ignorance, or pride of opinion, give them a false interpretation, because palpably conflicting with other positive declarations upon the same subject. For an example, Christ says of the wicked at the judgment: "These shall go away into everlasting punishment." Well, Paul was inspired to write: "Who shall be punished with *everlasting destruction.*" But, they say, that means everlasting preservation in suffering; well, if it does mean this, then the destruction, or preservation, will never come to an end; but, to show the fallacy of this prevarication, God inspired another prophet to write this: "Thou hast destroyed the wicked, thou hast put out their name, forever and ever; destructions are come to a perpetual end."—Ps. ix, 5, 6. Therefore, the everlasting destruction, call it what you will, has come to a perpetual end. It has ceased, with all the destructions. Their very names, have perished; God has put them out, forever and ever. Now, it is impossible to put out the names of men, as long as the men themselves exist. From these inferences, they conclude that the wicked suffer conscious agony, without end, and as this makes them live forever, they, therefore, give them eternal life, and as this implies immortal, *not* mortal life, the wicked are therefore pronounced to be immortal, though the Apostle was inspired to write: "God only hath immortality," and He has never promised to give this great boon to the wicked; but always to the righteous, as a reward for their suffering for His sake. Now, having given the wicked, immortality and eternal life, they then argue, that as they cannot cease to live, they cannot cease to suffer; therefore, their torments are endless. Such is the sophistry which weekly pours from the pulpits of the land; and we do not hesitate to say, that these same men would be ashamed to so pervert the teachings of any other book than the Bible, which, if they read it at all, they cannot but see that the least infraction, or change of God's Words, by His servants, in declaring even the national punishment pronounced against the wicked, invariably met with the severest punishment; where then, will such appear, who thus put light for darkness and darkness for light, when He makes inquisition who has declared, "Heaven and earth shall pass away, but My Words shall not pass away."—Matt. xxiv, 35. "For, verily I say unto you, till heaven and earth pass, one jot or one tittle shall in no wise pass from the law, till all be fulfilled."—Matt. v, 18.

The Immortality of the Soul Shown to be Absurd by the Word of God.

To expose the error that the soul is immortal, and that its glaring absurdity may be seen still further by every one, we have only to insert the qualifying word "immortal" before that of soul, where the latter is used in the Bible; for if it teaches that the soul is immortal, then, wherever the word soul occurs, that of immortal is implied. We will, therefore, thus supply it, in the following examples: "The (immortal) soul that sinneth, it shall die."—Ez. xviii, 4. Here, an immortal soul can die, which is an impossibility; for, to die, would show it to be mortal; not mortal, is what the word means. "But if the priest buy any (immortal) soul with his money."—Lev. xxii, 2. Here immortal souls may be bought and sold for money. Socrates thought it would be a difficult undertaking to catch his soul, which would be necessary, in order to deliver the strange merchandise to the purchaser. "The (immortal) soul of King David longed to go forth unto Absalom."—2 Sam. xiii, 29. Now, Absalom was dead, and the immortal soul of David longed to be dead also. "He made a way to His anger; He spared not their (immortal) soul from death."—Ps. lxxxiii, 50. Consequently, their immortal souls died; they were, therefore, mortal. "Their (immortal) soul melted because of trouble."—Ps. cvii, 26. "Whereas, the sword reacheth unto the (immortal) soul."—Jer. iv, 10. Cato says:

> "The soul secured in her existence,
> Smiles at the drawn dagger
> And defies its point."

"'They have given their pleasant things for meat to relieve the (immortal) soul."—Lam. i, 11. If they had not possessed these pleasant things, their immortal souls would have starved for the want of food. "Fear Him which is able to destroy both (immortal) soul and body in hell."—Matt. x, 28. No, Christ, you are mistaken in your supposed power, for the soul is "indestructible." "And the multitude of them that believed were of one (immortal) soul."—Acts iv, 32. Here were a multitude of immortal souls, consolidated into *one.* "He which converteth the sinner from the error of his way, shall save a (immortal) soul from death."—James v, 20. No, James, it is a mistake, for the soul is deathless. "Yea, his (immortal) soul draweth near unto the grave."—Job xxxiii, 22. Then the immortal soul goes into the grave, and this proves it is *mortal.* "Because he hath poured out his (immortal) soul unto death."—Isa. liii, 12. "He, seeing this before, spake of the resurrection of Christ, that His (immortal) soul was not left in hell, (the grave.)"—Acts ii, 31. Here, Christ's soul was poured out unto death, and was dead in the grave, and would forever have remained there, had not the resurrection taken Him from it. "Though I were perfect, yet would I not know my (immortal) soul."—Job ix, 21. As the soul is the man himself, Job says, I would not know myself, though I were perfect. Such perfection would make Job so ignorant that he would not know himself. "My (immortal) soul is weary of my life."—Job x, 1. The soul, then, is not the life; but Job himself, being the soul, he was weary of his life. "And now my (immortal) soul is poured out upon me."—Job xxx, 16. "So shall they be life unto my (immortal) soul."—Prov. iii, 21. Life, therefore, is not the soul, for these were to be life to his soul. "For thou hast delivered my (immortal) soul from death."—Ps. lvi, 13. No, David, God could not have delivered your soul from death, for it is deathless. "Save me, O God, for the waters are come in unto my (immortal) soul."—Ps. lxix, 1. Do not be afraid, David; your soul is immortal, and, therefore, waters cannot drown it. "Let my (immortal) soul live, and it shall praise thee."—Ps. cxix, 175. This inspired prayer is without sense, for the soul is ever-living. "I have given the dearly beloved of my (immortal) soul into the hand of her enemies."—Jer. xii, 7. I have given the dearly beloved of my (immortal) self, is the idea. Hence, he himself is immortal; but as he himself died, he was, therefore, not immortal. "My (immortal) soul desired the first ripe fruit."—Mi. vii, 1. His soul could not have been immaterial, as it desired material food. "I will say to my (immortal) soul, (immortal) soul, thou hast much goods laid up for many years; take thine ease; eat, drink, and be merry."—Luke xii, 19. This man's (immortal) soul could eat and drink material food, and therefore was not an immaterial thing. "Yea, a sword shall pierce through thy (immortal) soul."—Luke ii, 25. Suppose it did, a sword couldn't kill, or in the least, wound an immortal thing. "But now our (immortal) soul is dried away."—Num. xi, 6. To dry a thing away, is to evaporate it into its elements; therefore, the soul may be unmade. "To slay the (immortal) souls that should not die."—Ez. xiii, 19. If the soul may be slain, it is not immortal. "So, being affectionately desirous of you, we were willing to have imparted unto you, not the Gospel of God, but also our own (immortal) souls."—1 Thess. ii, 8. The immortal soul was something, according to this, that might have been given to another. "And when he had opened the fifth seal, I saw under the altar the (immortal) souls of them (of the living—from among the living members of the church who were not slain) that were slain for the Word of God."—Rev. vi, 9. "And the second angel poured out his vial upon the sea, and it became as the blood of a dead man; and every living (immortal) soul died in the sea."—Rev. xvi, 3. The sea is a symbol of people. "And the waters which thou sawest, are peoples, nations, multitudes and kings." Under the pouring out of this vial, all these immortal souls died. "As it is written, the first *man, Adam*, was made a living (immortal) soul."—1 Cor. xv, 45. Yet the man, Adam, died. "And all the days that Adam lived, were nine hundred and thirty years, and he died."—Gen. v, 5.

We see by these absurdities, that the soul cannot be immortal, according to the teachings of the Scriptures. There are a very few instances in which the word soul means the same as that of spirit; but in almost every case, it is used to designate the whole living man, and is in perfect accord with God's definition of the word, the first time it was ever used. "And the Lord God formed man of the dust of the ground, and breathed into his nostrils the breath of life, and the *man became a living soul.*" There were eight souls saved in the ark from drowning—the eight persons of Noah's family. There were about three thousand souls—three thousand persons, added to the church on the Day of Pentecost. In fact, you may substitute persons for souls, in almost every passage in the Bible where "soul" occurs, and it will not change the sense, as it always signifies the living man himself, and not a part of him.

That the Spirit is Immortal, also Shown to be Absurd, by the Scriptures.

There is another class of interpreters who claim that it is not the soul, but the spirit, which is the immortal part of man; and, therefore, whenever the word spirit is used in the Bible, that of "immortal" is understood. In order to expose this error also, all we have to do is to supply the word "immortal," to that of spirit, making it read, immortal spirit. We may remark here, that we hold this to be an infallible rule of interpreting Scripture phrases, and leaves no work for the self-conceited pride of man's wisdom, "which is foolishness with God," and which is sure to be such, if it contradicts the "Word of God."

Webster defines "Spirit" thus: "*Esprit*, French." "*Spirito*, Italian." "*Espiritu*, Spanish." "*Spiritus*, Latin." The primitive sense is, to rush or drive, and signifies the wind in motion; to blow, to breathe. Hence, breath.

"All bodies have spirits and pneumatical parts within them."—Bacon. Therefore, it means disposition. A generous spirit. A revengeful spirit. "The ornament of a meek and quiet spirit." That which hath power or energy; the quality of any substance, which manifests life, activity, or the power of strongly affecting other bodies; as the spirit of wine, or of any liquor. To animate, or actuate or excite.

The word spirit is used in the Bible to signify every one of these phenomena, and if it means the immortal part of man, then it means the immortal part of every other animal—the animating, immortal part of every plant, and even the immortal energy of intoxicating wine, and even the chemical affinities of inanimate or inorganic bodies; each has an "immortal spirit."

We have seen that, in the case of Adam, his soul was the whole living man, while the wind, breath, air, or spirit, was only a part of his life. That all the animals, in common with Adam had the breath of life in their nostrils, is God's own declaration. "For yet seven days, and I will cause it to rain upon the earth forty days and forty nights; and every living substance that I have made, will I destroy from off the face of the earth; and the mountains were covered; and all flesh died that moved upon the earth, both of fowl, and of cattle, and of beast, and of every creeping thing that creepeth upon the earth, and every man, all in whose nostrils was the breath of life—of all that was in dry land died."—Gen. vii, 4, 21, 22.

Here was the breath of life in the nostrils of every creeping thing, as well as in the nostrils of man; therefore, every living beast, all cattle, and every insect, has the same breath, and in the same organs, as man, and if it is a part of God—the divine essence; in man, it is a part of God, and of divine essence, equally in every creeping insect upon earth. If it is an immortal spirit in man's nostrils, so is it the immortal spirit of the beast. It is also equally taught, that God *created* the lower animals. "And God created great whales."—Chapter i, 21. In the case of Adam, it is said, "God breathed the breath of life into his nostrils;" and does not say how he forced it into the other animals, but that does not alter the fact that they both had it equally, and both received it as the act of God, in their creation. Of course, these Scripture statements settle the question as to man's having an immortal spirit, or God-essence, which distinguishes him from the lower animals, or even the lowest animalcule that moves, or insect that creeps, upon earth, and leaves those who still hold to the heathen doctrine of the natural immortality of the soul, or spirit, the only alternative, of denying the Words of God.

But, to corroborate these statements of the creation, and expose the heathen notion of the immortality of the spirit of man, we proceed to consider a number of passages where the word spirit occurs, and qualify it by that of immortal. "Who knoweth the (immortal) spirit of a beast that goeth downward to the earth."—Ecc. iii, 21. "The (immortal) spirit of Egypt, shall fail."—Isa. xix, 3. "For the Lord hath poured out upon you the (immortal) spirit of deep sleep."—Isa. xxix, 10. "Thus saith the Lord God, He that giveth breath unto the people upon it, and (immortal) spirit to them that walk therein."—Isa. xlii, 5. "He formeth the (immortal) spirit of man within him." This shows that the spirit is a part of the living formation. "But He turned and rebuked them, and said, ye know not what manner of (immortal) spirit ye are of."—Luke ix, 55. "And behold, there was a woman which had a (immortal) spirit of infirmity eighteen years."—Luke xiii, 2. "The words that I speak unto you, they are (immortal) spirit."—John vi, 62. "Now we have received not the (immortal) spirit of the world."—1 Cor. ii, 12. "Or, if ye receive another (immortal) spirit which ye have not received."—2 Cor. xi, 4. "The (immortal) spirit in us lusteth to envy."—James iv, 5. "Ye have not received the (immortal) spirit of bondage."—Rom. viii, 15. "When the Lord shall have washed away the filth of the daughter of Zion, and shall have purged the blood of Jerusalem from the midst thereof, by the (immortal) spirit of judgment, and by the (immortal) spirit of burning."—Isa. vi,

4. "And it came to pass, as we went to prayer, a certain damsel, possessed with a (immortal) spirit of divination, met us, which brought her masters much gain by sooth-saying."—Acts xvi, 16. This was by holding seances. "The (immortal) spirit of God was in my nostrils."—Job xxvii, 3. "And as they thus spake, Jesus himself stood in the midst of them, and saith unto them, Peace be unto you; and they were terrified and affrighted, and supposed they had seen a (immortal) spirit. And He said unto them, why are ye troubled? and why do thoughts (such thoughts of heathenism) arise in your hearts? Behold My hands and My feet, that it is I myself, and not a (immortal) spirit; handle Me, and see; for a (immortal) spirit hath not flesh and bones, as ye see Me have."—Luke xxiv, 36—39. "When Jesus saw that the people came running together, He rebuked the foul (immortal) spirit, saying unto him, thou dumb and deaf (immortal) spirit, I charge thee, come out of him, and enter no more into him; and the (immortal) spirit cried, and rent him sore, and came out of him; and he was as one dead, inasmuch as many said, he is dead." —Luke ix, 25, 26. It seems from this, that a man may live, after he loses his immortal spirit. "And I saw three unclean (immortal) spirits, like frogs, come out of the mouth of the dragon, and out of the mouth of the beast, and out of the mouth of the false prophet; for they are the (immortal) spirits of devils."—Rev. xvi, 13, 14. These immortal spirits, looked like frogs, and were the immortal spirits of devils, but the devils themselves are also held to be immortal spirits. Hence, they were immortal spirits of immortal spirits; this is good spiritualism. "When the unclean (immortal) spirit is gone out of a man, he walketh through dry places, seeking rest, and finding none. Then

he saith, I will return into my house from whence I came
out; and when he is come, he findeth it empty, swept,
and garnished. Then goeth he, and taketh with himself,
seven other (immortal) spirits, more wicked than himself,
and they enter in and dwell there; and the last state of
that man is worse than the first."—Matt. xii,. 43, 44.
Here is a man who had eight immortal spirits, besides his
own, and the sequel showed that the more immortal spirits
a man had, the worse he was off. There can be no doubt
but that this man was a most wonderful medium. "Nor
was their (immortal) spirit in them."—Job v, 1. "There
was no (immortal) spirit in her."—1 Kings x, 5. Here are
some who have no immortal spirit at all, and others who
have quite a number each. The old dame, nature, was
not very discriminating, as well as somewhat partial, in
these instances of spirit distribution. Here we have the
foolish notion of immortal spiritualism exposed, so that it
would seem no man who believes the Word of God, can
hold to the opinion.

No Future Punishment for the Heathen.—The
Principle Stated.

We would not be doing justice to the subject of future
punishment, were we to pass in silence, an objection so
often and legitimately made against the indiscriminate punishment of the heathen, who had never heard the Gospel,
with those who had heard and rejected its offers. We
have seen that man was virtually in possession of eternal
life, when created, having free access to the "tree of life,"
which, if it had continued, would have enabled him to live
for ever; but by sin, he was excluded from this, and, con-

sequently, lost eternal life, and in that very day, "In Adam, all died." The temporal life of man was continued, that his posterity might have a second offer of eternal life. This is the fundamental principle of the Gospel, conceived by the Great God, urged on by His intense love for mankind, and the certain prospect of the accomplishment of His purpose in endowing all those who would accept of the offer upon the conditions presented, with eternal life. This provision and proposition is set forth in these striking words: "For God so loved the world, that He gave His only begotten Son, that whosoever believeth in Him, should not perish, but have everlasting life."—John iii, 16. It is clear from this, that all who do not comply with the condition, shall not have eternal life, but shall perish. We see, therefore, that by refusing the second offer of eternal life, they incur the penalty of the second death, just as surely as man once lost eternal life, in Adam.

Another inference from this doctrine, is, that those who never hear of Christ, cannot believe in Him, which belief, alone, gives the qualification for eternal life, and therefore they also must perish. Now, we propose to show that the perishing of this class of mankind is limited to the first death as already alluded to, and that when a heathen, in this qualified sense, goes into his grave, that ends his existence. Our only inquiry, as ever, is, "What saith the Scriptures?" And that servant which knew his Lord's will, and prepared not himself, neither did according to His will, shall be beaten with many stripes; but he that knew not, and did commit things worthy of stripes, shall be beaten with few; for unto whomsoever much is given, of him shall much be required; and to whom men have committed much, of him they will ask the more."—Luke xii, 47, 48. Both classes perish; but one with the first death, the few stripes; the other, with the many, the second death.

Mark the expression, "To whom men have committed much." A man preaches the Gospel of eternal life to another, who has never heard it before, and who has already suffered the first death, and if he rejects the offer, that makes him a candidate for the second death, and therefore, for the resurrection to damnation.

Paul said to the Jews, "Since ye judge yourselves unworthy of everlasting life, lo! we turn to the Gentiles."—Acts xiii, 46. "For we are unto God a sweet savor of Christ, in them that are saved, and in them that perish; to the one, we are the savor of death unto death, and to the other, the savor of life unto life." We go to them who are dead, the sufferers of the first death, and offer them everlasting life, which, if they reject, makes them subjects for the second death—" death *unto death*," the last of which, they would have escaped if we or some one else had not carried the light to them, and told them that God wanted them to become candidates for His eternal kingdom. We go to others, who also have temporary life, given for the very purpose that they might hear the Gospel; and make the offer of everlasting life, by accepting which, the preaching proves a savor of life unto life—temporal life unto eternal life. It is clear from this, that if men never hear the Gospel, their loss and suffering will be limited to the first death.

"For this is the condemnation, that light is come into the world."—John iii, 19. Again, "If I had not come and spoken nnto them, they had not sin; but now they have no cloak for their sin."—John xv, 22. These are Christ's own words to the Jews; and nothing can be taught clearer, than that they became sinners by refusing compliance with the offer thus made and imposed, as well as having incurred the consequent punishment of the second death. "The wages of sin, is death." "And the times of this ignorance God winked at, but now commandeth all men, every where, to repent; because He hath appointed a day, in which He will judge the world in righteousness, by that Man whom He hath ordained, whereof He hath given assurance unto all men, in that He hath raised Him from the dead."—Acts xvii, 30, 31. Here we see that the judgment is to proceed upon the principle of "righteousness," which would have been impossible with those who had never heard of Jesus and the resurrection, or the Gospel of Salvation. "For there is no respect of persons, with God; for as many as have sinned without law, shall also perish without law; and as many as have sinned in the law, shall be judged by law." Here, those who had never known of the law, are to perish without it, and if they had never heard of it, it could never have imposed any obligation; hence, they could not have violated its enactments or incurred its penalty; and who could, therefore, perish but once, and that was by the loss of everlasting life, as a consequence of Adam's sin; that is, a loss of access to the tree of life, including his posterity.

But now, having heard the Gospel of Jesus and the resurrection, which offers eternal life the second time, but if rejected, it criminates the rejectors, and renders them candidates for the "second death." "For where no law is, there is no transgression."—Rom. iv, 15. "For until the law, sin was in the world; but sin is not imputed, where there is no law."—Chapter v, 13. "For by the law is the knowledge of sin."—Chapter iii, 20. "Nay, I had not known sin, but by the law; for I had not known lust, except the law had said, thou shalt not covet."—Chapter vii, 7. As this is one of the commands of the Decalogue, it shows that the law about which Paul is arguing, is the moral and the ceremonial, and it is evident that the conclusion is, that the law is necessary, and a knowledge of the law, in order to bring sin or transgression into existence, and that transgression is necessary in order to incur penalty; and the whole of these Scriptures go clearly to show that God recognizes the principle, and righteously awards the losses and penalties accordingly.

THE HEATHEN SUFFER THE FIRST DEATH, BUT NOT THE SECOND.

The heathen, having lost eternal life by the fall of man, have once perished, and without a part in the resurrection to eternal life, which only comes through belief in Jesus Christ, will remain perished. The wages which is their due, is the first death. Those to whom eternal life, by Jesus Christ, is offered, and the offer is rejected, merit also the wages of sin, and in this case, it is the second death. That this principle is recognized in the resurrection, and none but saints and sinners are its subjects, and also that there are no sinners but those who have had the offer of life, and rejected it—have "done evil," is proved by the following: " Marvel not at this, for the hour is coming, in which all that are in their graves shall hear His voice, (the voice of the Son of Man,) and shall come forth; they that have done good, unto the resurrection of life; and they that have done evil, unto the resurrection of damnation."—John v, 28. All that have done good or evil, shall come forth, but not all men indiscriminately; those who had sinned without law, and to whom sin was not imputed, and therefore had done no evil, remained perished; or just as though they had never existed; but those who had the law, came forth to damnation, and are judged by the law, and again perish, and that without remedy. "This is the second death."

Daniel says, "Many of them that sleep in the dust of the earth shall awake; some to everlasting life, and some to shame and everlasting contempt."—Chapter xii, 2. It is not here stated that those who came forth were good and bad; but the same discrimination is made, by the expression, "Many, not all the dead, came forth." And indeed, none but transgressors could have been covered with shame, or held in contempt by others, for their rejection of life. It is also true, by Scriptural representations, that none are arraigned before the judgment-seat of Christ but the good and bad, and are judged out of the things written in the Books, which they had heard and violated.

Christ said, "The words which I have spoken unto you, they shall judge you in the last days." Those, therefore, who had never heard of these words, could not be thus judged. "And I saw the dead, small and great, stand before God; and the Books were opened; and another Book was opened, which is the Book of Life; and the dead were judged out of those things which were written in the Books. And the sea gave up the dead which were in it; and death and hell delivered up the dead which were in them, (this was the contents of the grave,) and they were judged every man according to their works, and death and hell were cast into the lake of fire. This is the second death. And whosoever was not found written in the Book of Life, was cast into the lake of fire."—Rev. xx. 12, 15.

There is a passage of Scripture used for the purpose of proving that the heathen can be saved, without knowing anything about the Gospel of Jesus Christ, but, of course, can teach no such sentiment, for it is positively declared, that "There is no name given among men, whereby we must be saved, but the name of Jesus Christ." Indeed, such a supposition arrays itself against the whole plan of God's redemption of man and the world. The passage is this: "For when the Gentiles, which have not the law, do by nature the things contained in the law, these having not the law, are a law unto themselves, which show the work of the law written in their hearts, their conscience also bearing witness, and their thoughts, the meanwhile, accusing or else excusing one another, in the day when God shall judge the secrets of men by Jesus Christ, according to my Gospel."—Rom. ii, 14, 16. This last sentence shows, that the Gentiles alluded to, are not the heathen we are contemplating, who never heard the Gospel, but the Gentile Christians, in contrast to the Jews, and to whom Paul had preached the Gospel, and by which they were to be judged. These were said to be, "Not under the law, but under grace, they were of faith, and to whom Christ had become the end of the law." For ye are not under the law, but under grace. "The law is spiritual," so it had become to the Gentile Christians, "The work of the law written in their hearts." That the Gentile Christians were made free from the law, by the righteousness of faith, or that, having the faith of Abraham, it was counted to them for righteousness, was a subject upon which Paul dwelt almost continually, especially with the Jewish Christians, many of whom claimed that the Gentile Christians should keep the laws of Moses, and even that they should be circumcised; but his argument was, that "Christ became the end of the law to every one that believed;" and that the intent of the law was not answered by outward performance, but reached to the motives and intentions. The demands of the law, "Thou shalt not kill," were satisfied, if no outward murder was committed, but the Gospel version of the law, widened up its claims and penalties, and declared, "He that hateth his brother, is a murderer."

The law of the Sabbath was satisfied, if those under it worshiped God one day in seven; but the spirit of the law, written in the heart, demands that its subjects shall worship God every day and hour. "Whatsoever ye do, do all to the glory of God."

The Conditions of Salvation or Eternal Life.

It would be inappropriate to close this discussion, without pointing out the conditions upon which the offer of eternal life is made, and consequently, eternal death avoided. In order to do this, let us suppose a natural occurrence, though in all its elements a very uncommon one. Here is a man who has lived a great many years in a certain community; a man of character, wealth, and honor; but from circumstances beyond his control, has suddenly lost his wealth, health, and honor, as well as his friends, as the usual result. His disease is contageous, and by the public authorities, he has been taken to a pest-house. During all this time, there also lived in the same community, a wealthy physician, who could certainly cure every one afflicted with this disease. There are certain conditions with which every patient must comply, who would avail themselves of his skill. One is, he must be applied to in person; another is, that no compensation must be offered for his services; another is, that all other physicians and aids must be abandoned. He was generally known as the poor man's physician; that he was very seldom applied to by the rich, and among whom he had a very poor reputation, and thus was he esteemed by our once rich patient, and this was well known by the physician.

The principle reason why the rich did not apply to him, was, that he would not permit them to pay for his services, or to depend upon any degree of help in effecting the cure, either of their own, or that of others, and this was too humiliating. That he had treated this physician with such cold indifference for so many years, while living neighbor to him, increased the embarrassment of the sick man, in making the application. But in his extremity he resolves to call the physician, in hearty compliance with all the conditions, and puts it into execution.

There is implied in the application, confidence, or faith, in the ability and willingness of the physician to cure him; sorrow or repentance for his former ill-treatment; confession that he is utterly unable to cure himself; and humility that he is thus so poor, weak and depending, and that, too, upon one whom he had so persistently despised, and upon whom now rests his only hope, and that of mere mercy and grace; but he is encouraged when he reads this physician's advertisement, thus: "Ho, every one that thirsteth, come ye to the waters; and he that hath no money, come ye, buy and eat; yea, come, buy wine and milk without money and without price. Wherefore do ye spend your money for that which is not bread, and your labor for that which satisfieth not? Incline your ear and come unto Me; hear, and your soul shall live."—Isa. lv, 1—3.

No sooner was the application made, than the sufferer felt the vigorous throbbing of the vital forces through his system; the disease was gone, and the man was made whole; he leaves the chains of the pest-house, and walks forth a new man; and the first gush of his nature, is that of unutterable gratitude to his bountiful benefactor. Instead of the humiliation being a permanent affliction, as he supposed, it has resulted in an exaltation, of which he had no previous conception. *This is conversion to Christianity.*

In his boundless beneficence, the physician now puts a Will into his hands, and tells him to search it, and intimates to him that his work of cure is not yet done, but that he proposes to so perfectly reorganize his entire nature that it can no more be sick, or suffer pain; neither can it die any more, and this will be eternal life. "Search the Scriptures, for in them ye think ye have eternal life, and They are they which testify of Me."

The Place and Nature of the Promised Reward.

He also intimates, that in this "Will," there is a grand estate, in a new country, that shall have no end, and to which he is the heir, and that the Will can never be changed, as the Testator is dead; and that sealed the covenant; but He is risen again, in order to prepare the inheritance, and raise up the man again, to eternal life; all of which the patient finds true, by searching the Will, and he concludes, that if his physician can effect such a cure as now courses through his physical, moral, and mental nature, that He can also repair it to such perfection that it will live forever; and in his new-born hope, he cries out, in ecstasy, "Blessed be the God and Father of our

Lord Jesus Christ, which, according to His abundant mercy, hath begotten us again unto a lively hope, by the resurrection of Jesus Christ from the dead, to an inheritance incorruptible and undefiled, and that fadeth not away, reserved in heaven (New Heaven and New Earth) for you, ready to be revealed in the last time, wherein we greatly rejoice."—1 Peter i, 3, 6. This same Apostle, says, "Nevertheless, according to His promise, we look for a New Heaven and a New Earth, wherein dwelleth righteousness."—2 Peter iii, 13. "Hearken, my beloved brethren, hath not God chosen the poor of this world, rich in faith, and *heirs of the kingdom* which He hath promised to them that love Him?"—James ii, 5.

He has now searched the Will, and found that the eternal life and eternal inheritance it describes, are to be given graciously, and upon the simple conditions with which he had already complied, provided he was not to take the future work into his own hands, and out of those of his benefactor. "To him that overcometh, will I grant to sit with Me in My throne."

The man that was so poor, so sick, so helpless, is now rich—rich in faith, or in hope of inheritance, the very anticipation of which, makes him happier than though he possessed everything the present world affords. Riches is only a feeling, only in the anticipation.

Dr. Edward Beecher's Criticism on the Words "Aei" and "Aionios."

We gladly quote the following criticism from Rev. Dr. Beecher's book, just published, entitled, the "History of Opinions on the Scripture Doctrine of Retribution." The object of the author has been to ascertain what the Scriptures of the Old and New Testament, distinctly teach upon the subject, both by the etymological and general sense, which the words *aei* and *aionios* conveyed to the popular mind, among cotemporary and previous writers, as the sense in which they were understood by the Fathers of the Church.

This book is not a history of his own opinions, but of the opinions of the chief authorities of the Christian Church on this great subject, and in answer to inquiries, he dispassionately confesses that his long years of study have led him to abandon the narrow, popular interpretation. He maintains that the Fatherly character of God is fully revealed to us by Jesus Christ, and that the beneficence and justice of His character is irreconcilable with the popular Calvinistic view of the destiny of the vast majority of the human family.

Does *aionios* mean endless? Mr. Beecher gives the definition of *aion* in "Damm's Lexicon," thus: "Continuance, or duration to the end; any perpetuity." It denotes properly, the whole duration of the life of man, the duration of mortal life. Hence, to finish one's *aion*, is to die. The words *aei on*, denote existing perpetually, and without any intermission, *until the end comes*."

In this word, the idea of physical life is at first predominant and exclusive, and afterward is united with ideas of time, outward state, and moral character; but in more than five centuries, in such writers as Homer, Heriod, the Orphic Hymnists, Sophocles, Euripides, Pindar, Herodotus, Xenophon, and Thucydides, we do not come to the idea of eternity. Another change was necessary in order to arrive at this idea, which was this: The original idea of life was subordinated and disappeared, and ideas of time alone took possession of the whole ground, and *aion*, instead of denoting life, came to denote time. Thus, Marcus Aurelius, in his twelve books of "Meditations," uses *aion* twenty times, and always denotes by it, some form of time, and never life.

By a natural transition, it acquired the sense of eternity, and *aionios*, its cognate adjective, of eternal past time, is past eternity; all future time is future eternity; all time, past, present, and future, is absolute eternity. On pages 148 and 149, there is abundant proof that *aionios* is the precise equivalent of *olam* in the Old Testament; that it is always used instead of the latter Hebrew word in the Septuagint, and that its sense in the Old Testament is not, and cannot be, endless, because it is applied constantly to that which is limited and temporary. Dr. Beecher unreservedly adopts the logical conclusion of Professor Taylor Lewis, who, like himself, is an orthodox clergyman, that *aionios*, as used by Christ, means "pertaining to the age or world to come, taking world in the time sense." So that, with Dr. Lewis, he translates the much-debated passage, thus: "These shall go away into the punishment of the world to come." Professor Lewis adds, "That is all we can etymologically or exegetically make of the word, in this passage," and "so it is ever translated in the old Syriac version, where the one rendering is still more unmistakably clear." " These shall go into the pain of the *olam*, (the world to come,) and these into the life of the *olam*, (the life of the world to come.)" Toward the close of the work, Dr. Beecher says, "On the common basis, the doctrine of endless punishment, in my judgment, admits of no defense."—Page 299.

Reason for Introducing these Opinions.

We have introduced these criticisms of Dr. Edward Beecher and Dr. Lewis, not because they contain a single idea, which, as we have seen, is not clearly taught in our version, by letting the Author explain, in one passage, upon any subject, what He means in another; but because they are good, as authority, so far as qualification in understanding the import of the words, in original manuscripts translated into our version, as any others in the schools of the world; and what gives their views upon this subject additional weight, is the conclusion reached, that endless misery can no more be defended by any words in the original, than in their renderings in our Bible, when such a conclusion is in opposition to the doctrines of their own cherished denominations and systems of theology. Indeed, the very antithesis of the words contained in any passage upon the subject, shows the common theology upon the doctrine of future punishment to be error. Take the passage above alluded to, and read it according to the rendering the endless-misery theorists claim for it, and we at once see the absurdity of such ideas. "And these shall go away into everlasting (eternal) life, and the righteous into life eternal."

Here is another passage, and of a class which distinguishes between life or existence, and death and evil, or misery. "See, I have set before thee this day, life and good, and death and evil."—Deut. xx, 15. Here, the life is conscious existence, and the good is the happiness; on the other hand, the death is the extinction of conscious existence, and the evil, the conscious suffering while dying;

the one member being the opposite of the other; which, according to the common theory, should read the word "death," life." "See, I have set before thee, life and good, and 'life' and evil."

Take the text in 2 Thess., i, 9, which explains in what the everlasting punishment of Matthew consists, and all is plain. "Who shall be punished with *everlasting destruction*." But the common theology is, that destruction does not mean the cessation of conscious existence; then it means its opposite, which is conscious existence. Now read the passage with this rendering: "Who shall be punished with everlasting life," while in the passage in Matthew, the reward of the righteous is "everlasting (eternal) life." Both words, it is claimed, mean the same.

Who cannot see that "the wisdom of man is foolishness with God," and that our version of the Bible, by letting its Author explain its own meaning, brings it within the comprehension of the common English reader, and which the critical doctors could also understand, were it not that their pride of opinion makes them the teachers of God Almighty. "Thus saith the Lord God, woe unto the foolish prophets, that follow their own spirit, and have seen nothing."—Ez. xiii, 3.

OBJECTION, "THIS VIEW TAKES AWAY THE MOTIVE TO REPENTANCE."

There is one other objection to the extinction of the wicked, which we wish to expose before closing this little book. It is said, it takes away the motive to become Christians, and we have heard many professed Christians say, if they believed the wicked would only be burned up, and that would put them out of conscious existence, they would not be Christians at all. In regard to such, we cannot avoid the conviction that they have never had the least conception of Christianity, and that the fear of endless misery never yet made a man a Christian, being an utterly inadequate motive in itself, and a gross perversion of the Gospel. In order to vindicate this assumption, let us change its terms to suit the hypothesis. "For God so loved the world that He gave His only begotten Son, that whosoever believeth in Him, should not perish, but have everlasting life."—John iii, 16. Its antithesis, "For God so loved the world that He gave His only begotten Son, that whosoever believeth in endless misery, shall be saved." Such a condition leaves Christ out altogether; what a horrid substitution.

The final commission was, "Go ye into all the world, and preach the Gospel to every creature. He that believeth, and is baptized, shall be saved; but he that believeth not, shall be damned."—Luke xvi, 15, 16. The new theological rendering is this: "Go ye into all the world, and preach to every creature; he that believeth in *endless misery*, shall be saved; and he that believeth not in endless misery, shall have endless misery."

This is a very simple creed; and that a great many ministers of *this Gospel*, and their deacons, and cooperating lords over God's heritage, honestly believe in it, as their only hope of salvation, is evident from the fact that they keep in their cages of unclean birds, all kinds of workers of iniquity, and tolerate every phase of belief; and will even grant a fair trial to a thief, and never question the piety of a rich worldly man, yet those who disbelieve in endless misery, are cast out without trial, and with the utmost precipitation, to prevent the contagion from spreading, as they vainly hope. A man may believe Christ is nothing more than a man, and that He never died, but lived right on from the sham crucifixion, and instead of rising from the dead, and out of the grave, He never was there. He may believe he has the kingdom of God in his stomach, or in the cavities of his heart; indeed, he may entertain any foolish notion he pleases about anything taught in the Bible, if he is all right—and to be orthodox, is to be right—on the endless-misery question. He is a good sheep; but those who are wrong here, are all heretical goats, no matter if there is not a blemish upon their Christian character or spirit; endless misery must be believed, or the heretic be damned. It seems to us, that men of such merciless spirits, must be infatuated, in contending for *endless* misery, for their only hope is that there is no punishment at all for the wicked persecutors of Christ's saints.

Such a citizen of a country, says, I have no patriotism or love of country, and I only obey its laws because I fear the punishment of their violation. I would defraud, steal, and murder, every day, were it not for the misery, the punishment; this is my highest motive. He further says, I believe in endless misery, and from the consideration of avoiding its torments, I became a Christian, and if the wicked are only burned up, I never would have been one, for I would have been willing to have suffered as much as that, rather than to have made such great sacrifices of money and revengeful feelings as I have done, since I became a church member; and all that has restrained me has been "endless misery;" this is my theme of delight, and in heaven I shall shout, "Unto endless misery, be glory."

And now that I am here safe, I will tell you, Lord, frankly, I was not, in heart, your loyal subject, and did not love the restraints of your laws; and if you had failed to have made it the Gospel of endless misery, you could never have counted me in your company. I am here, therefore, because you were such a tyrant that you threatened to keep me forever alive, on purpose to torment me, and that man whom I met in the judgment, who also believed you were such a character, and in endless misery, too, saying, " I know thee that thou art an hard man, reaping where thou hast not sown, and gathering where thou hast not strewed; and I was afraid, and hid thy money;" was very foolish in not joining the church and submitting to your hard rule, to avoid endless misery, which you know I believed so fiercely, that I helped to excommunicate all who did not believe it. Will the Lord say to him, "Well done, good and faithful servant; enter into the joy of thy Lord."

On the supposition that it is future punishment which constitutes the motive for repentance, and to become Christians, and that its degree in kind and length of time, makes the motive stronger or weaker, gives us the conclusion that God must threaten and inflict, not only endless misery, but in the severest degree of which He is capable; and to threaten, and not perform, would be utterly inconsistent with His character. From the human standpoint, let us suppose a case of such suffering.

Here we have a sinner who has been resurrected from the dead, and, of course, is in his bodily existence. In the first place, his nerves are strung to the highest possible degree of sensitiveness, so that the least touch of fire would throw his whole system into the most excruciating paroxysms, and yet he is enveloped in flaming fire, without the least intermission, and that it is consuming, not only every vital organ, but every part of his being. To keep him in conscious existence, God has made him of such a nature that there is a perpetual reproduction of all the parts, equal to the consumption. He must be afflicted with every disease of which we know men are capable; Liver complaint; inflamation of the brain, and of the vital organs, and especially every muscle, with inflamatory rheumatism; every tooth aching with the greatest intensity; eating cancers covering every part of his body, and all infected with gnawing worms.

In addition to all this suffering, they are made with an infuriated disposition, to torment each other, and with every instrument of torture they are able to invent. Besides this, they are surrounded by implacable demons, excelling them in strength and inventive skill, whose only satisfaction consists in tormenting others, and especially these human victims of their malice. These, we can conceive, are capable of the employment of a system of infernal machinery, entirely beyond our imagination. Though none of these beings are naturally immortal, yet by the direct and perpetual work of God, are kept in a state of living, conscious existence, when, if He would take off His hand, they would die in a moment.

Here is a degree of suffering, which, even within the reach of human conception, God is able to inflict; and what heathen god of Tantalus possesses such enormous cruelty? But God is capable of contriving as much greater instruments of torture than man can comprehend, as He is greater than man; but not until He has exhausted His skill in finding out enginery of misery, and His power to inflict it, has He accomplished that which would constitute the strongest motive to induce repentance, if the principle that punishment is such motive, and the sequence of which is, that it is weaker or stronger in proportion to the degree of the punishment. Such is the doctrine of endless misery.

God's Oath in Contrast to the Picture of Horror.

In infinite contrast to such a picture of horror and omnipotent tyranny, we hear the voice of God speaking thus: "Have I any pleasure at all, that the wicked should die? saith the Lord God; and not that he should return from his ways, and live? Cast away from you all your transgressions, whereby ye have transgressed; and make you a new heart and a new spirit; for why will ye die, O house of Israel? for I have no pleasure in the death of him that dieth, saith the Lord God; wherefore, turn yourselves, and live ye."—Ez. xviii, 22, 31, 32.

Now, if God does not take pleasure in the death here spoken of, and which is the second death—the opposite to life—as the consequence of final refusal to live, then He must prolong His own misery by prolonging that of the sinner; and if this is to be endless, so He himself must suffer without end; but as it is the nature of God, as well as of all sentient beings, to seek His own happiness, He must therefore put an end to every source of His own discomfort, and therefore to the finally impenitent. "They shall be as though they had not been."—Obadiah 16, is the pronounced destiny of the wicked.

We close the discussion by exposing two heresies, either of which is fatal to Christianity, as the logical conclusions of the heathen doctrine of the immortality and immateriality of the soul.

THE HEATHEN DOCTRINE OF FUTURE PUNISHMENT DENIES CHRIST'S DEATH AND RESURRECTION.

The Papal scholastic divines, who adopted the heathen philosophic system of Aristotle, calling it theology, taught that all souls, and, of course, that of Christ, were immortal and immaterial, and therefore could never die; that it was the living, thinking, feeling being who dwelt in the body, just as a man dwells in a house; that Christ's death was in appearance only, and was simply a separation. It is true, that only the sect called the Nicolaitanes, professed this doctrine, or drew this legitimate conclusion; but no thinking mind could come to any other. The body was matter and mortal, and therefore no part of the living, thinking, feeling inhabitant.

That the living inhabitant did not die, they are particular to tell us where He went and what He did on the day of the crucifixion. One of these places was Paradise. That He was just as much alive and intelligent, as though He had never hung on the cross. As the body was no part of the life, of course it could not die, as nothing but life can die; therefore, no part of Christ died, and if no part of Him died, no part of Him could have risen from the dead. Hence, Christ never died, and never rose again to save sinners; and as upon these two events, according to the Scriptures, depend the salvation of men, therefore, according to this heathen doctrine, all men are lost.

If nothing but the material body died, then nothing but such a quantity of matter, without sense, thought or feeling, for these belonged to the immaterial, immortal soul, constituted the sacrifice for the sin of the world. In fact, this theology defined Christ's resurrection body to be of such a spiritual nature—so free from matter, that it could pass directly through a material door, without making the least rent. Here, then, we have the damnable heresies, growing out of the heathen doctrine of the immortality and immateriality of the soul, that denies Jesus Christ ever died, or rose from the dead. The dead saints are, therefore, all perished, and the living ones without the least hope of future existence or salvation.

We close by the remark, that if the "*eternal life*" is the gift of God to the saints, from which all the wicked are excluded, then there will come a time when they (the wicked) will cease to live, therefore, "Endless misery" is impossible.

"But now, being made free from sin, and become servants to God, ye have your fruit unto holiness, and the end, everlasting life; for the *wages of sin, is death;* but the gift of God is *eternal life, through Jesus Christ, Our Lord.*" —Rom. vi, 22, 23. Eternal happiness implies eternal life, in which to enjoy it, while eternal misery also implies eternal life, in which to suffer; which idea, reverses the whole counsel of God upon the subject.

An Appeal to the Corruptors of God's Words.

How have the cunning priests defiled
Thy Holy Words, and men beguiled?
The wise, in wisdom's high conceit,
Foul them beneath unhallowed feet.
Behold thy creatures lofty flight
Above the stars, in arrant might,
Teaching God what His Words doth mean,
And better plans, He had not seen.
Go hide thyself, thou worm of earth,
Nor revel thus, in giddy mirth ;
Learn first that thou dost nothing know,
And thus thy real wisdom show.
If high exalted thou wouldst be,
First vail thee in humility.
Go learn of Him, the great, but meek,
Hear the words the lowliest speak ;
Thee, in due time, shall He exalt
Upon His throne, without a fault.

THE END.

THE Sword of Truth.

Christ and Paul—Socrates and Plato—

WHICH?

*Future Punishment:
Biblical, Scientific and Philosophic.*

*Endless Misery and Purgatorial Restoration:
Myths of Heathenism.*

WHAT IS TRUTH?

"See, I have set before thee this day, life and good, and, death and evil."—Deut. xxx, 15.

BY

Prof. THOMAS MITCHELL,
OF
THE BIBLICAL AND SCIENTIFIC COLLEGE,
BROOKLYN, N. Y.

AUTHOR OF

"*Philosophy of God and the World,*" "*The Gospel Crown of Life,*" "*The Old Paths,*" "*Philosophy of Spiritualism, (No Spirits,)*" "*Household Tragedy,*" (*A Poem,*) "*Voices from Paradise,*" (*A Poem,*) "*The True and False Church,*" "*Commentary on the Book of Revelation,*" "*Civil and Religious Liberty,*" "*Darwinism and the Geological Antiquity of Man, refuted by Philosophy, Science and the Bible,*" "*Phonetic and Stenographic Short Hand,*" "*Water Baptism No Ordinance of the Christian Church.*"

BROOKLYN, N. Y.:
H. R. STARKWEATHER, PRINTER, 235 ADELPHI STREET.

1878.

Deacidified using the Bookkeeper process.
Neutralizing agent: Magnesium Oxide
Treatment Date: August 2005

PreservationTechnologies
A WORLD LEADER IN PAPER PRESERVATION

111 Thomson Park Drive
Cranberry Township, PA 16066
(724) 779-2111

www.ingramcontent.com/pod-product-compliance
Lightning Source LLC
Chambersburg PA
CBHW020301170426
43202CB00008B/456